A Pocket Guide to

HAWAI'I'S
TREES AND SHRUBS

Text and Photographs by
H. Douglas Pratt, Ph. D.

Museum of Natural Science
Louisiana State University
Baton Rouge, Louisiana 70893

Botanical Consultant:
Rick Warshauer
U.S. Geological Survey
Biological Resources Division
Hawaii National Park, Hawaii

MUTUAL PUBLISHING

FOREWORD

You may well wonder why an ornithologist would write a book about plants. One obvious reason is that one cannot enjoy birds without at least a superficial acquaintance with the vegetation in which they live. Also, my biological education included several courses in botany, so I can claim at least some training in the subject. My research specialty, the Hawaiian honeycreepers, are noteworthy for the phenomenon of coevolution with native plants, in which the shapes of birds' bills have evolved along with the shapes of flowers so that the birds pollinate the flowers as they feed on the nectar. (For a discussion and illustrations of this subject, see A *Pocket Guide to Hawai'i's Birds*.) But my real reasons for writing this guide are more specific. Some readers will know that I have a second career as an illustrator of natural history books. When I made my first visit to Hawai'i in 1974 to begin the field work I needed to illustrate a field guide to Hawaiian and tropical Pacific birds, I knew little about local plantlife. Upon my return home, I did a series of paintings of native birds in what I thought were natural settings based on photographs from my trip. The following year, I showed my painting of the scarlet and black 'I'iwi to a botanist friend, and asked what the plant was that I had chosen for the background. The not unkind but rather condescending reply was "It looks like guava." To my horror, I had painted a spectacular native bird in a plant that not only is not native to Hawai'i, but which could easily be called a weed! From that point on, I made it my business to learn what I could about Hawaiian plants. My work on the bird field guide, which was finally published in 1987, so piqued my curiosity that I made Hawaiian birds the focus of my doctoral research and began returning to the islands annually to gather data. I financed my field work with artwork, which included a series of paintings of rare native birds for the State Foundation on Culture and the Arts. Those paintings required serious attention to native plants for the backgrounds, and I began taking reference photographs for use in my Baton Rouge studio.

By the time I completed my dissertation in 1979, I had learned enough about Hawai'i to begin a sideline as an ecotour leader which continues to the present day. Birds are not always around, and sometimes finding a rare one involves a lot of sitting and waiting. Plants, on the other hand, are always there, rain or shine, and can provide a great deal of enjoyment for a birder waiting for a Maui Parrotbill or an 'Akikiki to appear. Leading nature tours gives me a unique perspective on what plants occur in the places people visit regularly, what plants people notice most, and what they want to know about them. I was constantly frustrated by the fact that no single reference covered the most commonly seen trees and shrubs in any comprehensive way. There were many small guides (see For Further Information, p. 128) to forest plants, shoreline plants, exotic tropical plants of parks and gardens, rare plants, or plants of specific small localities, but who wants to carry a library in a backpack? At some point, I realized that my collection of photographs could be the basis for just the kind of guidebook I had needed myself, and I began filling as many gaps as I could. You hold the result in your hand. This book is, in a sense, a tree guide for birders, but it should serve equally well for anyone interested in the natural world but who lacks the time or interest to delve into technical botany. It should not be regarded as a primary reference but rather as an introduction. I am proud to say that it is the most comprehensive popular guide to Hawaiian woody plants yet published. It will enable you to identify nearly all of the trees, shrubs, large ferns, and woody vines you see growing in the wild without having to translate technical jargon or consult half a dozen less complete books. My original goal was to include all plants in a single volume, but as the material grew, that goal became unrealistic. A pocket guide to Hawai'i's smaller plants is in preparation. I hope this book will enhance your enjoyment of natural Hawai'i and encourage you to learn more about the special nature of these beautiful islands.

ACKNOWLEDGMENTS

This book would not have been possible without the kind assistance of several "real" botanists. In particular, Rick Warshauer of the United States Geological Survey Biological Resources Division at the Mauna Loa Field Station deserves much of the credit for correcting what would have been some embarrassing gaffes. However, he did not review the entire finished manuscript, so any remaining errors are mine alone. In the field, Rick also taught me a great deal about both native and introduced plants on both Maui and the Big Island. On O'ahu, Patrick Conant, Sheila Conant, and David McCauley provided information and logistical support during the final stages of this book's development. Keith Unger of the McCandless Ranch Ecotour in Kona and David Kuhn of Terran Tours, Kaua'i, both provided helpful information and logistical support in the field. Others who over 2 decades provided various kinds of help include Phil and Andrea Bruner, Ken Clarkson, Reggie and Susan David, Steve Hess, James D. Jacobi, Jack Jeffrey, Jaan Lepson, Bob and Leilani Pyle, C. J. and Carol Ralph, J. Michael Scott, Rob and Annarie Shallenberger, Tom Snetsinger, Charles van Riper, and Dave Woodside.

Library of Congress Catalog Card Number 97-70285

ISBN 1-56647-219-9

First Printing, January 1999
Second Printing, March 2000
2 3 4 5 6 7 8 9

Design by Angela Wu-Ki

Mutual Publishing
1215 Center Street, Suite 210
Honolulu, Hawaii 96816
Ph (808)732-1709
Fax (808)734-4094
Email: mutual@lava.net
www.mutualpublishing.com

Printed in Thailand

TABLE OF CONTENTS

INTRODUCTION

THIS IS A FIELD GUIDE IN THE TRADITION OF THE LATE ROGER TORY PETERSON, WHO PIO-NEERED THE CONCEPT OF "FIELD MARKS" FOR THE IDENTIFICATION OF BIRDS AND LATER APPLIED IT TO PLANTS. THE PETERSON SYSTEM INVOLVES IDENTIFICATION BY OVERALL APPEARANCE COUPLED WITH SPECIFIC FEATURES BY WHICH ONE CAN SEPARATE AN UNKNOWN ORGANISM FROM SIMILAR SPECIES. IDENTIFICATIONS CAN BE MADE WITHOUT KNOWING EVERY DETAIL. TYPICALLY, PLANT IDENTIFICATION GUIDES DEPEND ON FEATURES THAT CAN ONLY BE SEEN IN THE HAND, SUCH AS FLOWER AND FRUIT STRUCTURE. SUCH THINGS ARE EASIER TO ASCERTAIN FOR PLANTS THAN THEY ARE FOR ANIMALS, BUT MAY NOT ALWAYS BE PRESENT OR VISIBLE. EVEN WITHOUT THEM, A KOA TREE CAN BE IDENTI-FIED FROM A CAR AT 55 MPH, AND KUKU'I GROVES ARE OBVIOUS FROM RIDGES MILES AWAY. CERTAINLY IT IS FASCINATING TO STOP AND COUNT THE STAMENS OR MEASURE THE PETIOLES, BUT IN MOST CASES IT IS NOT NECESSARY IF ALL ONE WANTS IS A NAME. THIS

IS A VISUAL GUIDE, AND THE PHOTOGRAPHS ARE THE MOST IMPORTANT FEATURE. THE TEXT PROVIDES ONLY THOSE DETAILS NECESSARY TO CONFIRM AN IDENTIFICATION AND SEPARATE THE PLANT IN QUESTION FROM SIMILAR SPECIES, ALONG WITH SELECTED OTHER FACTS INTENDED TO BROADEN THE OBSERVER'S APPRECIATION. FOR DETAILED BOTANICAL INFORMATION, NATURALISTS AND BOTANISTS IN HAWAI'I NOW HAVE AN EXCELLENT REFERENCE IN THE AUTHORITATIVE 2-VOLUME *MANUAL OF THE FLOWERING PLANTS OF HAWAI'I* (SEE FOR FURTHER INFORMATION), BUT THIS DICTIONARY-SIZED WORK IS HARDLY A FIELD GUIDE. I HAVE DRAWN HEAVILY ON THE *MANUAL* AS A SOURCE OF INFORMATION, AND I COULD NOT HAVE COMPLETED THIS GUIDE WITHOUT IT. FOR FERNS AND INTRODUCED CONIFERS I HAVE RELIED ON A VARIETY OF OTHER SOURCES, ESPECIALLY LITTLE AND SKOLMEN'S *COMMON FOREST TREES OF HAWAII*. AN AUTHORITATIVE MANUAL OF HAWAIIAN FERNS AND THEIR ALLIES IS A PARTICULARLY PRESSING NEED.

COVERAGE

This book is a guide to larger plants, most of which are "woody." The term "shrub" is defined very broadly to include woody vines as well as some very large herbaceous plants. Some decisions as to what to include were purely arbitrary. This is also primarily a guide to plants growing in the wild, including Hawaiian endemics, Polynesian introductions, and naturalized modern immigrants such as escaped garden plants, trees spreading from forestry plots, and shrubby weeds. Whether a plant is growing on its own or was planted is not always obvious, however, so Appendix 1 presents a selection of commonly seen garden plants that may appear to be wild but which are not known to be naturalized in Hawai'i. The text covers those species that the average amateur naturalist in Hawai'i, either resident or visitor, is most likely to see as well as some rare native trees and shrubs of special interest that may be seen only in cultivation or in remote areas reachable only with considerable effort. Although this book includes more species of wild trees and shrubs than any other popular guide, it is far from complete. Hawai'i's birds number in the hundreds, but the plants run into the thousands; no small book can cover them all. Many native trees or shrubs share a single Hawaiian name but are actually groups of several similar biological species. In some such cases, only one or a few examples are shown. Examples include alani (*Melicope* formerly *Pelea*), pilo (*Coprosma*), kopiko (*Psychotria*), hāhā (*Cyanea*), ōhā (*Clermontia*), loulu (*Pritchardia*), 'akia (*Wikstroemia*), 'akoko (*Chamaesyce*), and others. Those who want to sort out the various species in these groups will need to consult the more technical literature.

ORGANIZATION

Most laymen have little understanding of plant classification. Habitat is an obvious and easily understood feature of any plant, so this book groups plants together that are likely to grow in the same places. Within each habitat section, similar-looking plants are often placed together, but sometimes other criteria are more important. The habitats are presented in the order most people are exposed to them. Nearly everyone in Hawai'i lives near the coast or in towns and cities, and most visitors will go to a beach resort first. So this guide begins at the beach (makai) and moves inland (mauka). Most resorts, as well as the city of Honolulu, lie in dry "rain shadows" on the leeward sides of the islands, so dry lowland habitats are presented first. Hawai'i's lowlands are dominated by non-native plants, but look perfectly natural to the uninitiated. Hawai'i's artificial secondary rainforests (Section V) are so natural-looking, in fact, that they have been used in numerous "jungle" movies including *Raiders of the Lost Ark* and *Jurassic Park*. True native habitats, and in particular virgin rainforests (Section VII), are now mostly confined to remote areas high in the mountains. These spectacular forests are accessible by road only in a few places such as Koke'e State Park on Kaua'i and Hawaii Volcanoes National Park on the Big Island. Montane forests are the uppermost habitat on Kaua'i, O'ahu, Moloka'i, and Lana'i, but East Maui and the Big Island of Hawai'i are high enough to have a tree line, subalpine scrub vegetation (Section IX), and barren alpine zones (Section X). Both islands also have dry montane open forests on their leeward slopes and relatively recent lava flows. The easiest places to observe these habitats are the national park and Saddle Road on Hawai'i and the crater section of Haleakalā National Park on Maui. (Don't let anyone tell you it isn't a crater; it isn't a *caldera* but it *is* a crater!)

Habitats are not discrete areas; many plants grow in a variety of places. Perhaps the best example is 'ōhi'a-lehua, Hawai'i's most abundant native tree. It is one of the most ecologically variable trees known. It grows as a low shrub in montane bogs, as a pioneer on recent lava flows, as a small tree in dry scrublands and on coastal cliffs, and as the dominant canopy tree in native rainforest. But 'ohi'a is an exception; most plants confine themselves to a fairly narrow ecological zone. Those few native species that, like 'ohi'a, are characteristic of more than one habitat are illustrated or discussed in more than one section of this book. Even with other species, the observer should be aware that nature abhors sharp lines, and habitats usually merge gradually along their boundaries. Such transitional areas are known as ecotones, and they may include plants from two rather different habitats. Also, plants can be artificially moved and may grow in a new place but not be able to become established there in the long run. For example, breadfruit trees are a frequent sight along rural roads, and the trees were brought to the islands by the first Polynesian colonists, but the species is not considered naturalized because Hawaiian breadfruit trees are sterile. If they never produce seed, how can they become established in the wild? Consequently, when you see a large breadfruit tree you can be certain that someone planted it as a cutting. (This explains why Captain Bligh could not simply gather breadfruit seeds but had to remain in Tahiti to grow the trees in pots. The long sojourn led to the infamous mutiny on the *Bounty*.) Because vegetation grows rapidly in the tropics, abandoned homesites may look very natural and be indistinguishable from surrounding countryside, but breadfruit trees are sure indicators.

Many botanists who study Hawaiian plants are disdainful of introduced species and consider them all weeds unworthy of attention. That attitude is understandable, but the novice has no way of knowing what plants are native and which are introduced. Plants do not carry little signs that say "endemic" or "alien," and all plant communities in Hawai'i today have elements from a variety of sources. Therefore, little attempt has been made to segregate native plants from aliens brought to the islands by people. The origins of Hawaiian plants are important and interesting (see code system below), but plants that share the same habitat are grouped together regardless of origin.

FORMAT

The text is organized like that of A *Pocket Guide to Hawai'i's Birds*. There are no "species accounts" in the traditional sense; the plants are discussed in narrative fashion. The illustrations appear as close to the text comments as possible. If you do not find the plant's picture on the same or a facing page, look one page before or after. At its primary mention, a plant's vernacular names are boldfaced. Following the vernacular names, the italicized scientific name is given in parentheses along with the origin code (see below) and a number indicating the plant's botanical family (Appendix 3). When more than one example of a group of species that share a single vernacular name are shown, they are differentiated by numbers.

PLANT NAMES

The early Hawaiians named most of the plants they encountered and continued to do so into modern times as long as Hawaiian was widely spoken. Many of these names continue in popular use in the islands today. In this book, Hawaiian plant and place names are written with orthography that includes the glottal stop (written as an upside-down apostrophe), a consonant that does not appear in English, and the macron, a horizontal line over vowels that indicates stress. Use of these spelling devices is encouraged in Hawai'i today in everything from street signs to newspapers. Without them, correct pronunciation of Hawaiian words is much more difficult. In this text, the few orthographic exceptions are found in official names such as Hawaii Volcanoes National Park. For many Hawaiian plants, especially endemic species, the Hawaiian name is the only vernacular name in use. Many such names have entered the English language as loan words; "ohia" and "koa" now appear in standard English dictionaries (unfortunately without the glottal stops and macrons). Other plants have both English and Hawaiian names. In those cases the English is given first, followed by the Hawaiian. The choice of names is a matter of personal preference when several alternatives are available, and in a few cases I have had to create an English name. Vernacular names of plants are not capitalized because they have not been standardized to the extent that bird names have, and they vary widely from place to place.

Scientific names, on the other hand, are standardized even though they may differ in various publications. Theoretically, all organisms have one correct and unique scientific name, which can be determined based on a series of rules such as the Law of Priority, if all the facts are known and everyone agrees on relationships. Of course, differences of opinion on the latter point are common among scientists. Scientific names of species always have two italicized words, the first one capitalized (the genus) and the second one (the specific epithet) not capitalized. (In older botanical literature, specific epithets called patronyms, based on people's names, were often capitalized.) Unlike zoologists, botanists routinely include the author's name, not italicized, as a third part of the scientific name. Because of space limitations, only the genus and species are given herein. For scientific names and classifications, this book follows the *Manual of the Flowering Plants of Hawai'i* and, for tree ferns and introduced conifers, U. S. Department of Agriculture Handbook No. 679 (Little and Skolmen, 1989).

ORIGINS OF HAWAIIAN PLANTS

When the first Polynesians landed in the Hawaiian Islands about 1,500 years ago, they found a pristine archipelago that had evolved in the most extreme isolation on the planet. The animals and plants were descendants of chance arrivals from across 2,500 miles of inhospitable ocean. Over the millenia, they had evolved into an array of species unique to the islands. The Polynesians brought with them the plants and animals they used for food and fiber along with some accidental hitchhikers and weeds. After European contact, this trickle of alien organisms into the islands became a flood that continues to the present day. As a result, the modern Hawaiian flora reflects its human population: an amalgam of native species and immigrants from all over the world. This guide uses the following single-letter code to indicate each plant's origin.

E = endemic. Endemic species evolved in the Hawaiian Islands and are found nowhere else.

I = indigenous. Indigenous species colonized the Hawaiian Islands before the arrival of humans and still grow naturally elsewhere.

P = Polynesian. Plants introduced by ancient Polynesian settlers can be regarded as native in the same sense that the Hawaiian people themselves are so regarded. They are not, however, endemic or indigenous.

A = alien. Alien species are those that have become naturalized in the Hawaiian Islands since European contact in the late 1700s. Some were purposely brought to the islands, but many are weeds that arrived accidentally.

F = forestry plantings. Many trees have been planted in the islands for reforestation or lumber production. Some have become naturalized, but many are in a limbo wherein they sustain themselves within the plantations but do not spread widely.

C = cultivated. Many plants thought of as typically Hawaiian, such as pineapples, anthuriums, and most orchids, exist in the islands only as garden or agricultural plants. Sometimes, especially in the case of ornamentals and fruit trees, they persist in abandoned homesites or old fields and cannot be distinguished readily from truly naturalized plants. A few of these are included in the main text rather than Appendix 1.

I.   BEACHES AND SHORELINES

An undeveloped Hawaiian beach lined with **beach naupaka** and **ironwood**. Kawailoa Bay, Kaua'i.

OUTER STRAND

🐚 Not much grows on the beach. Beach sand is an unstable substrate and the effects of saltwater are ever present. Only a few plants can survive such a harsh environment, but those that do are highly successful and tend to be widespread because their seeds are easily dispersed in sea water. Thus, most native Hawaiian beach plants are indigenous rather than endemic. One of the most conspicuous is **seaside morning-glory** or **pōhuehue** (*Ipomoea pescaprae*; I, 27), a purple-flowering woody vine found on tropical beaches around the world. The Latin species name means "goat foot," and refers to the double-lobed

seaside morning-golory/pōhuehue

leaf shape that resembles a cloven-hoof track. The typical morning-glory flowers bloom right down to the waterline. The most common shrub of the strand is known in Hawai'i as **beach naupaka** or **naupaka kahakai** (*Scaevola sericea*, formerly S. *taccada*; I, 39). This familiar plant has large smooth-edged leaves and white

beach naupaka/naupaka-kahakai

Sandy beach with **tree heliotrope**

tree heliotrope flowers

beach vitex/pōhinahina

coast sandalwood

flowers that mature to fleshy white fruits. The flowers are unusual in looking as if half is missing. Beach naupaka has a pantropical distribution, but it has several relatives endemic to Hawai'i's montane forests (see Sections VII and IX). Beach naupaka is very popular as a landscape plant in beach resorts. Another salt-tolerant shrub or small tree often planted around beach hotels is **tree heliotrope** (*Tournefortia argentea*; A, 13) with velvety pale green leaves and small white flowers in coiled strands. Although a recent arrival in Hawai'i, tree heliotrope is native to Pacific islands to the south and west. A low-growing clump-forming shrub of the open strand is the purple-flowered **beach vitex** or **pōhinahina** (*Vitex rotundifolia*; I, 75). Like many of Hawai'i's native coastal plants, this one is becoming increasingly rare as beaches are developed. One good place to see it is Polihale State Park on Kaua'i. Even rarer is **coast sandalwood** or **'ili'ahialo'e** (*Santalum ellipticum*; E, 67), a sprawling shrub with stiff,

Hawaiian dodder/kauna'oa

'ilima

pa'u-o-Hi'iaka

'akoko

leathery rounded leaves whose growth form is very different from that of typical Hawaiian sandalwoods. A good site for beach sandalwood is Makapu'u Beach Park, O'ahu. Look for **Hawaiian dodder** or **kauna'oa** (*Cuscuta sandwichiana*, E, 30) growing as a parasite on many of these plants on all islands except Kaua'i. This unusual plant lacks chlorophyll entirely and its yellow twining stems look like piles of spaghetti. It is especially common along the shoreline between Ma'alaea and Lahaina, Maui.

THE BEACH FRINGE

Just behind the open beach, often in rocky places or on lava, one can find several other low-growing native shrubs. A common yellow flower is **'ilima** (*Sida fallax*; I, 44), used to make a very popular lei. The plant is so well known that two of Honolulu's taxi companies (Ilima and Sida) were named for it, perhaps because of the taxicab-yellow flowers. 'Ilima can be a creeping ground-cover on rocky shores or an upright shrub inland. Often growing with it is **pa'u-o-Hi'iaka** (*Jacquemontia sandwicensis*; E, 27), another woody morning-glory with very small pale blue or violet flowers and 1-inch oval, smooth-edged leaves. Hi'iaka was the younger sister of Pele, the volcano goddess, and the name means "skirt of Hi'iaka." **'Akoko** (*Chamaesyce degeneri*; E, 35) is another creeping shrub of rocky shores. Its nearly round red-tinged leaves that clasp the stem closely distinguish it from other species of 'akoko found in different habitats. It can be found in widely scattered localities throughout the islands. Much rarer than any of these is another sprawling woody plant called **'ōhai** (*Sesbania tomentosa*; E, 36). Its compound leaves and elongated red or orange pealike flowers are distinctive. This endemic is an endangered species but can be found on the hillside above the wave-washed lava at South Point on Hawai'i and at Kaena Point on O'ahu. In dry coastal habitats on Kaua'i one may find the showy yellow flowers of **Rock's Kaua'i hibiscus** (*Hibiscus calyphyllus = rockii*; A or E, 44). It is a popular garden plant in Hawai'i and was once thought to be endemic, but many botanists now believe it is actually an alien species from Madagascar. Its sprawling growth form distinguishes it from the other yellow hibiscus in Hawai'i.

'ōhai

Rock's Kaua'i hibiscus

coconut/niu

SHORELINE FOREST

🐚 Very few trees can tolerate the seaside environment but those that do are ubiquitous behind Hawai'i's beaches. **Coconut** or **niu** (*Cocos nucifera*; P, 80) has almost become a symbol of Hawai'i and other tropical islands, but its wide distribution is largely the work of humans. The tree

coconut flowers and young fruit

ironwood/paina

tropical almond/false kamani

tropical almond growing over salt water. 'Anini Beach Park, Kaua'i.

is believed to have been brought to Hawai'i by ancient Polynesians for whom it was a major source of food, fiber, and thatching material. Coconut is by far the most abundant palm in Hawai'i today and is easily distinguished from the rare native fan palms (see Section VII) by its pinnate (i. e. arranged like a feather) leaves and from planted date palms (see Appendix 1) by its smooth bark and different overall shape.

Many Hawaiian beaches are lined by what looks like a conifer, complete with small "cones" and drooping "needles." This is the **ironwood** or **casuarina** (*Casuarina equisetifolia*; A, 21), native to the southwestern Pacific. Despite its appearance, ironwood is not related to pines. It bears two kinds of flowers, male ones at the tips of the "needles" (actually modified stems) and female ones at their bases. Ironwood is useful as a windbreak because of its salt tolerance, but it can become a nuisance and form dense stands that allow nothing else to grow. On windswept shores it can even grow as a stunted shrub or dense mat. Several other species of ironwood (see Appendix 2) have been introduced to Hawaii, but are not yet well established or widespread in the wild.

Often growing right at the water's edge is a more recently introduced coastal tree called **tropical** or **Indian almond** and locally

false kamani (*Terminalia catappa*; A, 26). It is easily recognized by its flat-topped growth form and broad leaves, a few of which are usually bright red. The 2-inch fruits have a stringy hull and an edible kernel but require a lot of work to open for rather little reward. Because of its attractive foliage, tropical almond is often planted as an ornamental around resorts and has become thoroughly naturalized, especially on lava shores. It is called "false kamani" in Hawai'i because of the vague resemblance of its fruits to those of **Alexandrian laurel** or "true" **kamani** (*Callophyllum inophyllum*; P, 25), a common beach tree of Polynesian origin. Kamani has showy white flowers, thick, waxy, simple leaves, and fruits the size and shape of a chicken egg. Kamani is often used in landscaping around Hawaiian resorts but also grows wild in beach forest.

Several smaller trees form the understory of beach forests. One of the most common is the West Indian **autograph tree** (*Clusia rosea*; A, 25), named for the fact that one can impress letters into the fleshy round leaves with a sharp stick and later these will heal over as brown writing against the green background. Autograph trees form dense thickets, especially along the north shore of Kaua'i. More widespread is **Portia tree** or **milo** (*Thespesia popul-*

Alexandrian laurel/kamani flowers

kamani fruits

autograph tree

Portia tree/milo flower

milo mature fruits

ānapanapa

seagrape

nea; I?, 44), with yellow, dark-throated, hibiscus-like flowers and smooth, heart-shaped leaves with long tips. Mature milo fruits are hard, woody, dark brown, compressed 1-inch globes. Because the seeds float well and are not killed by salt water, milo has dispersed widely to beaches of the Indo-Pacific, but it may have had human help in reaching Hawai'i. Another indigenous strand plant that disperses by seed flotation is **ānapanapa** (*Colubrina asiatica*; I, 62), found naturally from Africa to the Pacific islands. It is a low-growing shrub or climber characterized by shiny simple leaves with prominent longitudinal veins and half-inch brown dry fruits. Look for it along shorelines of Kaua'i, O'ahu, and Moloka'i. Very popular as an ornamental around resorts is the West Indian **seagrape** (*Coccoloba uvifera*; C, 60). It has round or slightly heart-shaped leaves often tinged red and produces white, grapelike fruits in dangling chains. Seagrape is very common and apparently spreading on its own, at least on windward O'ahu between Kahuku and Ka'a'awa.

OTHER COASTAL HABITATS

🐚 Shorelines in Hawai'i are not always beaches. Around muddy areas, such as the landward shores of coastal fishponds, the fleshy-stemmed **pickleweed** or **kulikuli-kai**

Pickleweed flats surrounding ancient Hawaiian salt pan. Hanapepe, Kaua'i.

(*Batis maritima*; A, 10) forms dense stands. The fleshy stem sections are edible and taste salty. A larger weedy shrub of the same habitat is **Indian pluchea** (*Pluchea indica*; A, 9). Indian pluchea (pronounced *ploo-key-a*) can be distinguished from the related sourbush (Section IV) by its smaller leaves with toothed edges. Much more conspicuous than its pale purple flowers are the fuzzy-looking dry fruiting structures that persist on the plant long after the white-tufted seeds have blown away. These "dead flowers" make Indian pluchea easily identifiable at a distance.

Although mangroves are native in Micronesia and as far east as Samoa, they never reached Hawai'i

pickleweed/kulikuli-kai

Indian pluchea

red mangrove showing prop roots

red mangrove seedlings attached to tree

oriental mangrove

button mangrove

on their own. Several species were introduced as soil stabilizers but those that are now naturalized have become a nuisance in coastal ponds used by endangered water-birds. The seeds of mangroves germinate while still attached to the parent plant, growing a long root that penetrates the mud when the young plant finally drops. Thus they spread widely and can completely choke a formerly open pond. The leaves of all mangroves are simple, smooth-edged, and leathery. **Red mangrove** (Rhizophora mangle; A, 63), the most widespread species in Hawai'i, is characterized by arching prop-roots and spreading yellow flower bases that remain around the germinating seedling. Growing with it in Kane'ohe Bay, O'ahu is **oriental mangrove** (Bruguiera gymnorrhiza; A, 63), which lacks the arching roots but produces aerial roots called pneumatophores that protrude vertically from the surrounding water. Oriental mangrove flower bases are red and appear to clasp the base of the growing root. The smaller **button mangrove** (Conocarpus erectus; A, 26) from tropical America and Africa has also spread from cultivation in a few places on O'ahu, Lana'i, and Maui. Its fruits form globular brown half-inch clusters.

FRESHWATER SHORELINES

🍃 Many of the plants that grow around coastal fishponds also grow around inland freshwater ponds and along rivers, but others are restricted to fresh water. The familiar **common cattail** (*Typha latifolia*; A, 86), naturalized from North America, grows along Kaua'i's Wailua River and around ponds on O'ahu. Its bladelike leaves and vertical brown seed heads are unmistakable. Originally planted as an interesting ornamental, **papyrus** (*Cyperus papyrus*; A, 81) is a giant sedge that grows in the water along the edges of ponds and reservoirs. It was used by ancient Egyptians to make paper. The feathery sprays of small branches atop a slender green stem characterize this unusual plant which can be seen around Honolulu's reservoirs, at Keahua Arboretum on Kaua'i, and around Waiakea Pond in Hilo. With a similar growth form is **umbrella-grass** (*Cyperus latifolia*; A, 81), another ornamental sedge that has spread from cultivation and now grows commonly along slow-moving Hawaiian streams and even canefield drainage ditches.

common cattail

papyrus

umbrella-grass

II.   LOWLAND DRY SCRUB

Kiawe scrub. Koko Head Regional Park, O'ahu.

MOST OF HAWAI'I'S POPULAR RESORTS ARE ON THE SOUTHERN AND WESTERN SIDES OF THE ISLANDS. THAT IS BECAUSE THESE AREAS LIE IN "RAIN SHADOWS." MOISTURE THAT ARRIVES ON THE NORTHEAST TRADEWINDS FALLS AS RAIN ON WINDWARD SLOPES LEAVING LITTLE FOR THE LEEWARD SIDE. MUCH OF THE VERDURE ONE SEES AROUND RESORT AREAS SUCH AS WAIKĪKĪ ON O'AHU, KIHEI AND KA'ANAPALI ON MAUI, AND KONA ON THE BIG ISLAND, IS SOLELY THE RESULT OF IRRIGATION. LEFT TO THEMSELVES, THESE AREAS ARE DESERT-LIKE OR EVEN BARREN. OF COURSE, FOR THE VACATIONER THIS MEANS THE BEST OF BOTH WORLDS: TROPICAL GREENERY UNDER NEARLY PERPETUAL SUN. BUT IT ALSO MEANS THAT THESE AREAS HAVE SEEN SO MUCH ECOLOGICAL CHANGE THAT LITTLE THAT IS TRULY NATURAL REMAINS. AWAY FROM THE RESORTS, THE LAND IS DOMINATED BY ALIEN TREES AND SHRUBS, THE NATIVE VEGETATION HAVING MOSTLY BEEN CLEARED IN ANCIENT TIMES.

TREES

🌿 Several members of the pea family, characterized by pinnate (i. e. arranged like a feather) compound leaves, are common in dry places. Beginning immediately at the edge of irrigated lawns and golf courses, **algoroba**, a tropical American tree related to mesquite and known locally as **kiawe** (*Prosopis pallida*; A, 36), dominates the landscape. It has very small once-compound leaves that fall during dry seasons and yellow caterpillar-like flower clusters. It is the only coastal dry forest tree that can form a canopy. Kiawe is armed with formidable thorns that can easily penetrate rubber flip-flops, as many a beachgoer has painfully learned. A smaller tree growing in dense thickets but not forming a canopy is **koa haole** (*Leucaena leucocephala*; A 36), one of the most abundant and conspicuous plants in Hawaii today. The Hawaiian name means "foreign koa." This weedy legume can be recognized by its small white pompom flowers, feathery twice-compound leaves, and persistent brown seed pods. Less common but widespread is **sweet acacia** or **klu** (*Acacia farnesiana*; A, 36) which is rather similar to koa haole, but has fragrant yellow instead of white flowers, hard rather than papery seed pods, and smaller,

algoroba/kiawe

koa haole

sweet acacia

23

indigo in bloom

indigo seed pods

more delicate leaves. **Indigo** (*Indigofera suffruticosa*; A, 36) was once a source of blue dye (the original coloring for bluejeans) but is now mainly a weed. It has once-compound leaves, spikes of small pink or red pealike flowers, and 1-inch, strongly upcurved seed pods crowded along the stem. The spectacular and unmistakable **royal poinciana** or **flamboyant** (*Delonix regia*; A, 36) is very popular in tropical landscaping worldwide and has spread into dry habitats near resorts in Hawai'i. When not in bloom, it can be identified by its twice-compound leaves much larger than those of koa haole. It is most often seen as an ornamental in towns and cities. Keahole Airport in Kona has a particularly nice display.

royal poinciana

kou

Dry scrub in Hawaii also has a few broad-leaved trees. **Kou** (*Cordia subcordata*; P. 13), a small tree with heart-shaped shiny leaves and shallowly tubular orange flowers, was introduced by the first Hawaiians. It is difficult to tell from a close relative, the West Indian geiger tree (see Appendix 1), widely planted in Hawai'i where it is called "kou haole," but not known to be naturalized. Kou haole has darker, redder flowers and rough-surfaced, rather than shiny, leaves. **Indian mulberry** or **noni** (*Morinda citrifolia*; P. 47), with its broad, simple, glossy, dark green leaves that stand out against the drab background, is conspicuous among the scrub on old lava flows. The leaves appear disproportionately large for such a small tree. Noni fruits are especially distinctive and con-

Indian mulberry/noni

structed like giant knobby mulberries. When ripe, the soft, waxy, yellowish white fruit may be as big as a grapefruit. A Polynesian introduction, it had many medicinal uses and was a famine food. To find out why the fruit was only eaten as a last resort, try sniffing a ripe one. The smell brings to mind rotten lye soap.

Hawaiian cotton/ma'o

'ūlei

'akoko

'ākia

NATIVE SHRUBS AND VINES

🦋 In a few places, remnants of the native dry scrub community remain. One of the more interesting of these is **Hawaiian cotton** or **ma'o** (*Gossypium sandwicense*; E, 44). It is a member of the same genus as commercial cotton, but with short, brown cotton fibers of little use. The flowers are yellow and their form reveals their relationship to hibiscus. An endemic member of the rose family is **Hawaiian hawthorn** or **'ūlei** (*Osteomeles anthyllidifolia*; E, 64), a shrub or scrambling vine found in dry places near the coasts of all islands and also in high elevation dry habitats. A good place to see it is near the recent Kalapana lava flows in Hawaii Volcanoes National Park. 'Ulei has small, rather stiff compound leaves, fragrant white flowers, and half-inch white berrylike fruits. Also growing on lava, especially near the sea, are several native shrubs known as **'akoko** (*Chamaesyce* spp.; E, 35). They have inconspicuous flowers and simple, smooth-edged opposite leaves. A species (*C. celastroides*) with elongated leaves typical of the genus can be seen at Kilauea Point National Wildlife Refuge on Kaua'i. (The round-leaved *C. degeneri* is discussed in Section I.) A rare shrub of dry rocky sites is **'ākia** (*Wikstroemia uva-ursi*; E, 72). It belongs to a group of about a dozen endemic shrubs or small trees of diverse habitats. The various species can be very

leadwort/'ilie'e

dodder laurel/kauna'oa pehu

difficult to tell apart, so the beginner is best advised to just call them all 'ākia. A more common and wide-spread dryland shrub is **leadwort** or **'ilie'e** (*Plumbago zeylanica*; I, 59) whose wide distribution in the world's tropics includes the Hawaiian Islands. Some have speculated that it came to the islands by hitchhiking on migratory shorebirds. Perhaps the most unusual plant in Hawai'i's dry habitats is **dodder laurel** or **kauna'oa pehu** (*Cassytha filiformis*; I, 42). In its viny growth form it closely resembles parasitic dodder (Section I) but differs in being partly photo-synthetic, with some green stems. Dodder laurel is much more common and conspicuous than Hawaiian dodder and usually grows further inland. It can be rather spectacular in places such as South Kona and Hawaii Volcanoes National Park and is a surprisingly popular lei plant. Another native lei flower conspicu-ous in dry habitats is **'ilima** (*Sida fallax*; I, 44), already discussed in Section I. Its flowers are usually a uniform golden yellow, but the varia-tion shown here is not uncommon.

Dodder laurel covering large trees. South Kona Forest Reserve, Hawai'i.

Two-tone flower variant of **'ilima**

Cuba jute or **broomweed**

false mallow

OTHER SHRUBS AND WEEDS

🐚 Be careful not to confuse 'ilima with several introduced members of the mallow family. **Cuba jute** or **broomweed** (Sida rhombifolia; A, 44) has similar but smaller, paler yellow, flowers. Its leaves are rectangular rather than broad-based. Broomweed also grows commonly in wetter habitats. Very similar flowers are also found on **false mallow** (Malvastrum coromandelianum; A, 44) which, like broomweed, grows more often in wetter habitats than true 'ilima. It has coarsely sawtooth-edged leaves that are usually slightly lobed at the base. Also often confused with 'ilima, and an acceptable substitute for it in leis, is **hairy abutilon** or **ma'o** (Abutilon grandifolium; A, 44). Hairy abutilon is also sometimes confused with Hawaiian cotton (above) and shares the Hawaiian name. The flowers resemble 'ilima but the petals are not lobed on their outer edge and the leaves are larger and heart-shaped, with the basal lobes usually overlapping. Another common yellow-flowered dry country shrub is **'uhaloa** or **waltheria** (Waltheria americana; I?, 71). It is found mainly in tropical America, but has been in Hawai'i since pre-European times and may be native. Its flowers are much smaller than those of the preceding species, and bloom a few at a time from fuzzy clumps encir-

hairy abutilon

cling the stems. The clumps (bracts) persist on the plant after the flowers are gone. Leaves of 'uhaloa resemble those of broomweed and false mallow, but look silvery because of a covering of fine hairs and have the lateral veins deeply impressed into the upper surface.

'uhaloa

III. LOWLAND WET FOREST

Forest of **hala**, **hau,** and **kuku'i**. 'Uma'uma Valley, Hawai'i.

AS WE LEAVE THE DRY HABITATS THAT SURROUND MOST HAWAIIAN RESORT AREAS AND MOVE TO THE WETTER WINDWARD SIDES OF THE ISLANDS OR INTO THE MOUNTAINS, THE DRY SCRUB GRADUALLY GIVES WAY TO GREENER LANDSCAPES. ROADSIDES BECOME LUSH WITH WILD-FLOWERS AND WEEDS, GREEN PASTURES ARE DOTTED WITH LARGE TREES, AND VERDANT VALLEYS ARE CLOTHED IN DENSE FOREST. BUT IT IS NEARLY ALL ARTIFICIAL. AS IN THE DRIER ZONE, ALMOST NOTHING REMAINS OF THE NATIVE PLANT COMMUNITIES.

TREES

🐦 Originally the dominant tree in this habitat, **screw-pine** or **hala** (*Pandanus tectorius*; I or P, 83) is less common today. Some local tour guides are fond of identifying it as "pineapple tree" for naive visitors because the large fruits do, indeed, look like pineapples at a distance (the "pine" in the English name recalls the resemblance). The tree itself is small and palm-like, with numerous proproots around the base of the trunk and long narrow leaves with saw-toothed edges arranged in a spiral pattern (hence the "screw" part of the name). In old Hawai'i, the leaves were used for thatching and for weaving *lau hala* mats (*lau* means leaf). The fruits break up into pieces called keys, the inner portions of which are edible and sweet but annoyingly stringy. The keys float and the seeds remain viable in sea water, so *Pandanus* may be indigenous to Hawai'i, but an equally likely possibility is that it was introduced by Hawaiians in ancient times. Hala can be found along any Hawaiian coastline, but tends to survive today mostly on steep cliffs.

In river valleys and along lowland streams, the dominant, and often only, tree is **sea hibiscus** or **hau** (*Hibiscus tiliaceus*; I or P, 44), which forms dense stands with tightly intertwined trunks. Do not

pandanus/hala

Pineapple-like **hala** fruit

sea hibiscus/hau

31

Dense thickets of **hau** along a lowland stream. Wailua River, Kaua'i.

confuse it with milo (Section I), a similar tree that never forms thickets and whose flowers never open as wide. The Hawaiians had many uses for hau wood and may have purposely brought the tree to Hawai'i, but it is a good natural island colonizer and is probably native. Hau is characterized by large heart-shaped leaves and ever-present 3-inch yellow flowers. Each flower lasts but a single day, opening yellow in the morning and gradually turning red or orange until it closes and drops. Despite its name, sea hibiscus often follows streambeds high into the mountains. Hau thickets often grow beneath a canopy of **kuku'i** or **candlenut** (*Aleurites moluccana*; P. 35). The State Tree of Hawai'i, kuku'i was brought to the islands by the first Polynesians who used the oil-rich nuts for lighting and for the most prestigious of leis. Only *ali'i* (royalty) could originally wear the polished black (or sometimes brown) nuts. Kuku'i nuts grow inside a leathery walnut-like husk. Kuku'i flowers are white and the leaves are distinctively shaped, rather maple-like, and very pale frosty green. The pale foliage makes kuku'i groves conspicuous against their darker surroundings.

candlenut/kuku'i

common guava

Pale green **kuku'i** trees trace a steep valley.
'Aiea Trail, O'ahu.

Blossoms of **common guava**

Roadsides in wetter areas are often dominated by **common guava** (Ps*idium guajava*; A, 51), introduced nearly 2 centuries ago. Ripe guavas look superficially like lemons and often litter the pavement where they are squashed by cars, revealing the bright pink interior. Guava trees are rather small and have simple leaves with prominent straight side veins, white brushlike flowers, and reddish brown smooth bark marked by irregular green patches. Guavas often form dense thickets and can be a nuisance despite their succulent fruit. A more recent arrival is the related **Java plum** (*Syzygium*

Java plum

octopus tree or schefflera

Hawaiian sumac/neleau

cumini; A, 51) which is very common in towns and cities as well as rural roadsides. Any driver in Hawai'i in the fall months is familiar with the olive-sized soft, dark purple fruits that stain parking lots and paint jobs. Java plum has white shaving-brush flowers, thick, shiny, smooth-edged simple leaves and pale bark. A conspicuous component of windward disturbed habitats is the **octopus tree** or **schefflera** (*Schefflera* =

Brassaia actinophylla; A, 7), familiar to mainlanders as a house plant. In Hawai'i, it grows to tree size and blooms profusely in sprays of red "octopus-arms." In some O'ahu valleys, it forms dense stands and is especially prominent around Kahana Bay. The palmate (= radiating like the branches of a palm) compound leaves resemble those of the much taller trumpet tree (Section V). One of the few native trees to persist in this habitat is **Hawaiian sumac** or **neleau** (*Rhus sandwicensis*; E, 4). It forms thickets on roadsides and in old fields and is most common on the Big Island's Hamakua Coast, but occurs in scattered localities on the other islands. Mainlanders will recognize the typical sumac compound leaves with toothed leaflets and conical flower and fruit clusters at the ends of stems. Younger leaves are characteristically tinged red.

VINES AND SHRUBBY FERNS

🍃 **Woodrose** (*Merremia tuberosa*; A, 27), a commonly cultivated woody vine, has spread into the wet lowlands in Hawai'i and become a choking weed in places. It is named for its dry fruits that look like wooden flowers. The real flowers are yellow morning-glories and the leaves are deeply palmately lobed. Woodrose vines can completely cover tall roadside trees, as they do along the highway between Lihu'e and Kalaheo on Kaua'i. Among the few remaining native elements in windward lowland habitats is the epiphytic **birdnest fern** or **'ēkaha** (*Asplenium nidus*; I, F2) which grows high or low supported by the branches of tall trees. Widespread in the tropical Pacific, this fern is unusual in having huge fronds that are single undivided blades. The name comes from the resemblance of the basal clumps to bird nests when viewed from below. Another lowland fern that is both an epiphyte and a ground-covering vine is **maile-scented fern**, better known as **laua'e** (*Phlebodium* = *Microsorium scolopendrium*; I?, F9). Whether this fern is native or alien is controversial. It was not documented botanically from Hawai'i until the 20th Century, but is prominent in Hawaiian folklore and culture. The deeply pinnately lobed leaves have the aroma of maile (Section VII) and are likewise used in leis. Laua'e is

woodrose

birdnest fern/'ēkaha

maile-scented fern/laua'e

very popular in resort landscaping and is a familiar sight along lowland highways. It is highly adaptable and grows on lava rocks near the ocean as well as in secondary forest.

IV. OLD PASTURES, WEEDY FIELDS, AND ROADSIDES

Rural landscape, Kapaʻa, Kauaʻi.

IN MANY PLACES IN HAWAIʻI, AREAS FORMERLY USED FOR AGRICULTURE, PASTURAGE, GOLF COURSES, OR OTHER PURPOSES HAVE BEEN LEFT TO GROW UP IN WEEDS THAT SPREAD IN FROM THEIR MARGINS. SOMETIMES, AS IN THE CASE OF OLD PASTURES, THEY MAY STILL BE IN USE BUT BE HEAVILY INFESTED WITH MUCH-DETESTED BUT DIFFICULT TO CONTROL WEEDS. SUCH HABITATS DO NOT FIT ANY OF THE "LIFE-ZONE" DEFINITIONS, CAN OCCUR ALONG THE COAST OR FAR INLAND, AND AT ANY ELEVATION. NEVERTHELESS, THERE IS A CERTAIN UNIFORMITY IN THE PLANTS THAT OCCUPY THEM. EVEN A FEW NATIVE PLANTS BELONG TO THE "WEED" COMMUNITY.

Flowers of **monkeypod**

Mature fruits of **monkeypod**

LARGE TREES

🌸 **Monkeypod** (*Samanea saman*; A, 36) is a popular shade tree in public parks and a prominent feature of old pastures. Everyone has noticed the sticky seed pods that often litter streets in Honolulu. The broad, flat-topped trees have pink shaving-brush flowers and twice-compound, glossy dark green leaves. Monkeypod is sometimes jokingly called "salad-bowl tree" because of the popularity of its dark wood for such purposes. Often confused with monkeypod is the **siris tree** (A*lbizia lebbeck*; A, 36). It has similar leaves but the flowers are greenish white and the seed pods are flat and papery. Also popular for pasture shade, probably most often

Flowers of **siris tree**

Mature fruits of **siris tree**

Mango tree showing reddish young foliage. Wailua Valley, Kaua'i.

Mango flowers

Ripening fruits of **mango**

growing accidentally from discarded seeds, is **mango** (*Mangifera indica*; A, 4), whose delicious fruits are much prized. Mango trees have a globular profile and long narrow leaves that form a very dense canopy. Young leaves are tinged copper-red, and identify mango trees at some distance. One of the most beautiful trees of the Hawaiian rural landscape is **jacaranda** (*Jacaranda mimosifolia*; A, 11), native to tropical America. It has feathery double-compound leaves and brown ear-shaped seed pods, but its most striking feature is large clusters of trumpet-shaped purplish blue flowers that bloom in spring and summer. Particularly good areas to see jacaranda include the slopes of Haleakalā, Maui, and the Pu'u Wa'a Wa'a area on Hawai'i. Often providing a beautiful color counterpoint to jacaranda is **silk oak** (*Grevillea robusta*; A, 61), an Australian tree with brushy orange flowers and peculiar fern-like leaves. Silk-oak has been planted on all islands for reforestation, and has spread widely on its own. A relative of silk-oak and a popular lei blossom is the Australian **kahili flower** (*Grevillea banksii*; A, 61), a small tree with distinctive silvery leaves deeply divided into narrow lobes. Its red flower clusters can be spectacular along roadsides and in old pastures. It is especially conspicuous between Anahola and

Jacaranda in full bloom. Pu'u 'Anahulu, Hawai'i.

Flowers and fruits of **jacaranda**

silk-oak

kahili-flower

Pods and flowers of **'opiuma**

Typical foliage of **'opiuma**

tamarind

papaya

Kilauea, Kaua'i. **Manila tamarind** or **'opiuma** (*Pithecellobium dulce*, A, 36) is a popular medium-sized shade tree that has also spread into disturbed dry habitats on all the islands. It has peculiar crowded leaves that conceal sharp thorns. At a distance, the leaves appear small and simple, but close inspection reveals them to be compound, branched like the letter Y, with a pair of leaflets on each branch. It is the only tree in Hawai'i with such leaves. 'Opiuma has inconspicuous white pompom flowers and curled, often rose-tinged seed pods that contain an edible pulp. The pods differ from those of true **tamarind** (*Tamarindus indica*; A, 36), the pulp of which is popular as a flavoring for drinks in some tropical regions. Tamarind is also often planted as a street tree in Hawai'i and may spread on its own. It has once-compound pinnate leaves and brown straight pods.

SMALLER TREES

A popular fruit tree that, like mango, may be spread by discarded seeds is **papaya** (*Carica papaya*; A, 19). This unusual-looking tree is somewhat palmlike (although not related to palms), with an umbrella of large, deeply lobed leaves shading a cluster of flowers or fruits that grow directly from the trunk. Papaya-growing is a major industry in Hawai'i today, but the tree grows wild in field edges at least on Kaua'i, Moloka'i, and Hawai'i. Single trees often persist at abandoned homesites on all islands. In the edges of pastures and fields on Kaua'i and O'ahu look for **macaranga** (*Macaranga tanarius*; A, 35), a small tree whose 5 to 6-inch leaves are unusual in being "peltate," i. e. the stem or petiole attaches in the middle of the blade rather than the edge. Macaranga flowers are green and inconspicuous in sprays under the leaves. Another tree with peltate leaves and inconspicuous green flowers is the **Ceará rubber tree** (*Manihot glaziovii*; A, 35) but its leaves have 3 to 5 radiating lobes. Ceará rubber tree, named for a place in Brazil, is prominent along the highway south of Honaunau, Hawai'i, but is also present on the other large islands. **European olive** (*Olea europaea*; A, 53) is best known as a fruit-bearing tree, but in Hawaii is usually planted as an ornamental. It is spreading from cultivation on some ranch lands of the Big Island and becoming a pest. It has simple, opposite leaves and familiar olive fruits.

In cooler upland areas, look for **angel's trumpet** or **nānāhonua** (*Brugmansia candida*; A, 70), a spectacular ornamental tree that sometimes spreads from cultivation. It has huge dangling white (or sometimes peach-colored) trumpetlike flowers that produce a wonderfully

macaranga

Ceará rubber tree

European olive

angel's trumpet

pepper tree

chinaberry tree

sisal

sweet perfume at night. All parts of the plant are poisonous if eaten. **Pepper tree** (*Schinus molle*; A, 4), with its weeping branches, compound leaves with very narrow leaflets, and red berries is a popular ornamental that has become naturalized around Pu'u Wa'a Wa'a on Hawai'i and in pastures on East Maui. In those and other pastures, often in gulches, one can find the **chinaberry tree** (*Melia azaderach*; A, 46) which is easily identified by its large, sparse-looking twice-compound leaves with toothed leaflets. The half-inch yellow globular fruits persist on the tree even after the deciduous leaves have fallen.

UNUSUAL PLANTS

🍃 Some large dryland plants are difficult to classify as either trees or shrubs. Unmistakable is **sisal** (*Agave sisalana*; A, 78), which was brought to Hawai'i as a potential fiber crop. It is now naturalized on all of the main islands. The cactus known as **prickly pear** or **pānini** (*Opuntia ficus-indica*; A, 15) was brought to the islands from Mexico probably as a food plant but its fruits never became popular and it eventually became a pest. It is now controlled by introduced insects. In the Poipu area on Kaua'i, look for the tree-sized **hedge cactus** (*Cereus uruguayanus*; A, 15). It was introduced as an ornamental and is now conspicuous on roadsides throughout the area. Its solitary flowers open at night like those of its smaller relative, the **night-blooming cereus** (*Hylocereus undatus*; A, 15), also well established around Poipu as well as on O'ahu and Hawai'i. Night-blooming cereus has fluted 3-part trailing stems that can form dense masses. In Honolulu, look for it on Roundtop Drive above Manoa Valley and on the outer slopes of Punchbowl Crater.

prickly pear

SHRUBS

🦋 One of Hawai'i's most widespread and conspicuous roadside shrubs is **Brazilian pepper**, known locally as **Christmasberry** (*Schinus terebinthefolius*; A, 4) because of its round red fruits that ripen during the winter months. The compound leaves resemble those of sumacs to which it is related. Despite its attractive fruits, Christmasberry is a terrible weed in pasturelands throughout the islands, often forming dense stands that support few other living things and occu-

hedge cactus

Christmasberry

night-blooming cereus

tagasaste

pukamole

tree tobacco

yellow oleander

py huge tracts of formerly useful agricultural land. **Tagasaste** or **cytisus** (*Cytisus palmensis*; A, 36), which came to Hawai'i from the Azores with Portuguese immigrants, is a much more benign pasture weed on the slopes of Haleakalā, Maui. Its white pea-like flowers resemble the yellow ones of native mamane (Section IX), and cytisus is sometimes called by that name. In ravines of the same area grows **maritime loosestrife** or **pukamole** (*Lythrum maritimum*; I, 43), one of the few native shrubs that does well in weedy situations. It is a low-growing, somewhat viny plant with small purple flowers and tiny simple leaves that look a little like those of pukiawe (Section IX). It has an odd native distribution: Peru and Hawai'i. In weedy places on O'ahu, Lana'i, and Maui look for **tree tobacco** (*Nicotiana glauca*; A, 70), a spindly small tree with green trunks and branches and small, trumpet-shaped yellow flowers. It is related to true tobacco (*N. tabacum*; not shown), also naturalized in the Hawaiian lowlands.

Many of the flowering shrubs that enliven the Hawaiian countryside today began as ornamentals. A good example is **yellow oleander** or **nohomālie** (*Cascabela thevetia*; A, 5), easily distinguished from other yellow-flowered shrubs by its trumpet-shaped flowers and long narrow simple leaves. It is now common in disturbed weedy places, especially in urban areas, on Kaua'i, O'ahu, and

Maui, but is more familiar as a decorative park or garden plant. Several different species in the pea (legume) family have taken the name "kolomona," which refers to King Solomon (no one knows why). All have showy yellow flowers and once-compound pinnate leaves. Originally, the name applied only to the indigenous *Senna gaudichaudii* (not shown) which is now rare. It has rounded leaflets and dangling papery seed pods. Another **kolomona** (*Senna septemtrionalis*; A, 36) has pointed leaflets and inflated seed pods that do not dangle. Both are found on all the main islands. On Kaua'i, O'ahu, and Maui, another "kolomona," better known as the **scrambled-eggs bush** (*Senna surrattensis*; A, 36), has spread into old pastures and fields. It is so named because its tight flower clusters resemble masses of scrambled eggs. It has denser foliage than other kolomonas and flat, papery seed pods that turn light brown. The ornamental Siamese cassia (Appendix 1), often planted along streets and in gardens, is similar but has larger, more open flower clusters and persistent black pods. The related **golden candle** or **candle bush** (*Senna alata*; A, 36) has its flowers arranged in vertical spikes. Although mostly seen in cultivation, it sometimes grows wild on O'ahu, Kaua'i, and probably Maui. Also in the pea family but never called kolomona is **Mysore thorn** or **wait-a-bit** (*Caesalpinia decapetala*; A, 36), a woody

kolomona flowers

kolomona mature seed pods

scrambled-eggs bush

golden candle

Mysore thorn

gorse

vine or shrub introduced to Hawaii as a hedge plant. Its recurved thorns on leaves and stems make one "wait a bit" when entangled. It has become quite common along the north shore of Kaua'i, where its terminal clusters of yellow flowers can be conspicuous, but is also present on other islands. Unlike the foregoing yellow-flowered legumes, Mysore thorn has doubly compound leaves. **Gorse** (*Ulex europaea*; A, 36) also has yellow pea-like flowers but very different foliage. Also first planted as a hedge plant, it has become a serious pest in upland pastures such as those along Hawai'i's Keanakolu Road above Hakalau Forest National Wildlife Refuge, where large tracts of good pasture have been lost. Nearly every part of the gorse plant has sharp spines, making the dense clumps nearly impenetrable, and control measures such as burning and herbicides have been relatively ineffectual.

Belt of **gorse** in pasturelands above Keanakolu Road, Mauna Kea, Hawaii.

OTHER WEEDS

🐚 One of Hawai'i's most conspicuous and easily identified roadside weeds is **castor bean** or **pā'aila** (*Ricinus communis*; A, 35), characterized by round palmately lobed leaves often tinged purple. Its yellow flowers are small and inconspicuous, and the fruits are 1-inch burs with soft spines. The seeds or "beans" are the source of a valuable oil, but their skin contains one of the deadliest poisons known. DO NOT EAT CASTOR BEANS under any circumstances! The quintessential weed in Hawai'i is the much-detested **lantana** (*Lantana camara*; A, 75) which has both mechanical and chemical defenses against being eaten by cattle. Despite the fact that it is thorny and stinks, lantana was brought to Hawai'i as an ornamental! But the admittedly attractive multicolored flowers hardly compensate for its other attributes. Lantana is easily dispersed by fruit-eating birds and today forms dense stands in dry or wet habitats throughout the islands.

Many other weeds are either spiny or poisonous. **Apple-of-Sodom** (*Solanum linnaeanum*; A, 70) is widespread but is particularly noticeable in pastures along Hawai'i's South Point Road. The stiff leaves are very prickly and the small flowers are purple. The 1-inch round yellow fruits cling to the dead stems long after the plant has died.

castor bean/pa'aila

lantana

apple-of-Sodom

balloon plant

Seeds of **balloon plant** ready to fly.

Another pasture weed is **balloon plant** (*Asclepias physocarpa*; A, 8), a milkweed whose prickles are restricted to the inflated seed pods. The pods eventually dry and split open, allowing the seeds to disperse on the wind via fluffy white "parachutes." It has small white flowers with the unusual "crown-and-skirt" shape characteristic of the family. **Kaliko** (*Euphorbia heterophylla*; A, 35), related to the familiar poinsettia (Appendix 1), is a roadside weed in drier areas. It lacks the showy red bracts, but the leaves subtending the inconspicuous flower clusters may be white or silvery at the base. **Sourbush** (*Pluchea symphytifolia*; A, 9) is probably the most widespread roadside shrub in Hawai'i today because it tolerates a wide range of environmental conditions. It resembles the closely related Indian pluchea (Section I) in having inconspicuous fuzzy-looking lavendar flowers that mature into conspicuous dry brown seed heads that persist on the plant for a long time. But sourbush grows in drier habitats and has larger elongated leaves that are neither leathery nor toothed on the edge. One of the most recent additions to Hawai'i's growing list of noxious weeds is the **ivy gourd** (*Coccinia grandis*; A, 29). Since 1986, it has covered large areas of O'ahu's wet lowlands and is rapidly overgrowing vacant land around Kailua-Kona on the Big Island. This aggressive vine has broadly arrowhead-shaped leaves with toothed edges, showy white flowers, and dangling, bright red 3-inch fruits.

kaliko

sourbush

ivy gourd flowers

Ripe fruit of **ivy gourd**

V. AGROFOREST AND SECONDARY RAINFOREST

Well-developed secondary rainforest. Mānoa Valley, Oʻahu.

IN HAWAIʻI, NEARLY ALL THE LEVEL LAND NEAR THE COAST THAT RECEIVES SUFFICIENT RAINFALL HAS BEEN USED FOR AGRICULTURE AT SOME TIME OR OTHER. ANCIENT HAWAIIANS, FOR OBVIOUS REASONS, LIVED MOSTLY IN THESE AREAS BECAUSE THEY COULD GROW CROPS NEARBY AND STILL OBTAIN FOOD FROM THE SEA. THE USEFUL TREES AND SHRUBS THEY PLANTED WERE ALLOWED TO GROW UP INTO A FOREST THAT BECAME THE NUCLEUS OF A SECONDARY RAINFOREST THAT TODAY LOOKS PERFECTLY NATURAL.

POLYNESIAN AGROFOREST

🐦 The Polynesian element in Hawaiian lowland forest is actually a remnant of an artificial forest type found on most inhabited Pacific islands. Known as agroforest, it is dominated by introduced plants useful to humans but not usually grown in gardens. Nevertheless, because the habitat has been present for many centuries, such forest shows little, if any, evidence of its human origin. An especially deceptive indicator of agroforest is **breadfruit** (*Artocarpus altilis*; C, 47), an often large and impressive "forest" tree. The fruits do not produce viable seeds, so breadfruit trees are propagated from cuttings. All breadfruit trees in Hawai'i, no matter how "wild" looking, were planted by someone. Breadfruit was (and still is outside of Hawai'i) very important in the Polynesian diet. The round green fruits are the size of cantaloupe and are ripe when a white sap begins to ooze from the outside. When fruits are absent, breadfruit is still easily recognized by its deeply lobed hand-shaped leaves. **Taro** or **kalo** (*Colocasia esculenta*; P, 79), whose roots are made into poi, was the other staple in the ancient Hawaiian diet. The large heart-shaped leaves were also cooked and eaten when young. The flavor is spinach-like, but do not try to eat taro leaves

breadfruit/'ulu

taro/kalo

raw; they must be cooked to break down oxalic acid crystals that otherwise produce a painful reaction. Then as now taro was usually grown in irrigated, closely managed fields such as those at Hanalei, Kaua'i. However, in wet areas of secondary rainforest, wild taro

elephant-ear/'ape

sugar cane

ti/kī

plants persist. More often seen in the forest is a larger relative, **elephant-ear** or **'ape** (*Alocasia microrrhiza*; P, 79), also known as giant or swamp taro, which does not need to grow in standing water. It's root is also used for poi. The Hawaiians also cultivated **sugar cane** or **kō** (*Saccharum officinarum* hybrids; P, C, 84). The sugar cultivated today bears little resemblance to Polynesian varieties, but still spreads into agroforest especially along roadsides in cane-growing areas. Grown mostly for its leaves was **ti** (pronounced *tee*) or **kī** (*Cordyline fruticosa*; P, 78), a small tree or shrub with a spray of long leaves at the end of a bare stem. It is a familiar house plant on the mainland, often taken home by visitors as a souvenir. The Hawaiians used the leaves, called *luau*, to wrap foods for cooking. The leaves are the namesake for the traditional Hawaiian feast and are also the wrapping for *laulau*, the "Hawaiian box lunch." The Hawaiians also brewed a weak alcoholic beverage called *'okolehau* from ti roots. However, a much more important intoxicant before European contact was made from the pulverized roots of **kava** or **'awa** (*Piper methystichum*; P, 57). In modern Hawaiian culture it has largely been replaced by beer, but is still important in Polynesia and Micronesia. 'Awa is a small tree with rather large heart-shaped leaves and odd-looking green branches that are swollen where the leaves attach. The words taro, ti, and kava came into English from other Polynesian languages, hence the differing Hawaiian names. Hawaiian culture also depended heavily on fiber plants such as **paper-mulberry** or **wauke** (B*roussonetia papyrifera*; P, 47). This small tree, native to eastern Asia, has been transplanted all over the world and occasionally grows wild along lowland streams in Hawai'i. The inner bark of wauke is the basic material of tapa cloth (*kapa* in Hawaiian). The familiar **common bamboo** or **'ohe** (B*ambusa vulgaris*; C, 84) was also a source of fiber as well as building materials. Like breadfruit, bamboo apparently never sets seed in Hawai'i and so technically cannot be considered naturalized, but it is nonetheless one of the most conspicuous and abundant plants in secondary rainforest. Usually growing at somewhat higher elevations than the preceding is **mountain-apple** or **ohi'a-'ai** (*Syzygium malaccense*; P, 51), a medium-size tree popular for its elongated apple-like fruits. Its bright red "shaving-brush" flowers resemble those of the native ohi'a-lehua (Sections VI-VII), but they grow along the branches underneath the leafy canopy.

kava/'awa

paper mulberry

bamboo

mountain-apple

Flowers of **avocado**

Ripening fruits of **avocado**

liliko'i flowers

POST-CONTACT FOOD PLANTS

🍃 Soon after European contact, many new fruiting plants were brought to the islands and now are important components of secondary rainforest. Don Marin, a Spanish immigrant of the early 1800s, introduced papaya, mango, prickly pear, and guava, discussed in previous sections, as well as **avocado** (*Persea americana*; A, 42), a common understory tree today. Avocado has long, simple, smooth-edged leaves that have few distinctive characteristics. When the familiar rough-skinned fruit or terminal sprays of greenish yellow flowers are present, identification is easy. A somewhat later introduction was **passionfruit** or **liliko'i** (*Passiflora edulis*; A, 55) which grows on a vine that may climb high in roadside trees. The white and purple flowers are very showy and the smooth-skinned egg-shaped fruits can be either yellow or purple. Less well-known fruits introduced in the 19th century include two relatives of mountain-apple, the

yellow **passionfruit**

previously discussed Java plum (Section III), and **rose-apple** (*Syzygium jambos*; A, 51), which has conspicuous pale yellow brushlike flowers (much larger than those of other fruit trees in the myrtle family) and pinkish round 2-inch fruits. The simple glossy leaves are larger and longer than those of Java plum, but are rather similar to those of the **cinnamon tree** (*Cinnamomum verum*; A, 42), a recent introduction on Kaua'i, O'ahu, and Maui. Cinnamon's glossy simple leaves are yellow or reddish when young and have 2 prominent longitudinal side veins in addition to the midrib. Crushed leaves are strongly aromatic but do not smell particularly like cinnamon, which comes from the dried bark. Grown in Hawai'i mainly as a curiosity, this tree is spreading rapidly and could easily become a bad weed. It is now the dominant understory tree in Nu'uanu Pali State Park, O'ahu. **Coffee** (*Coffea arabica*; C, 65) has been grown in Hawai'i since the 19th century, but few expect to see

rose-apple

Rose-apple leaves and fruit.

coffee

cinnamon tree

macadamia nut

it growing wild in the rainforest. Nevertheless, in many places, such as Huleia Valley on Kaua'i, it is a common component of the understory. It can be distinguished from native members of the coffee family, many of which also have orange or red fruits, by its wavy-edged leaves. Wavy-edged leaves also characterize **macadamia nut** (*Macadamia integrifolia*; C, 61), another important crop tree in Hawai'i. Its white flowers and walnut-like fruits grow in long dangling clusters. Whether macadamia nuts are truly naturalized is problematical, but in regions where they are grown the trees are often found in secondary forest near orchards.

ORNAMENTAL TREES

🐦 Most of the trees of Hawai'i's secondary rainforest discussed so far originated as garden plants. At least for those introduced since European contact, their spread into the wild was more or less acciden-

African tulip tree

African tulip tree with yellow-orange flowers

African tulip tree typical flowers

tal. Today, many lowland forests are dominated by trees introduced purposely for their beauty or interest. Probably the most spectacular and noticeable of all is the **African tulip tree** (*Spathodea campanulata*; A, 11), also called flame tree. A magnificent tall tree with compound leaves and large clusters of bright red or golden tulip-shaped flowers, it is common in city parks and gardens, but also is now one of the dominant canopy trees of secondary Hawaiian rainforest such as is found in deep ravines along the Big Island's Hamakua Coast. Often growing with it there and around Hilo is the **king palm** (*Archontophoenix alexandrae*; A, 80), a native of Australia. King palm has a very straight trunk topped by a green shaft below the leaves (formed by the leaf sheaths) and bright red fruits with pale stems in hanging clusters just below the green sheaths. The only other pinnate-leaved palm growing wild in Hawai'i is coconut. Native palms are all fan-leaved. Also in windward Hawai'i as well as other places, the distinctive palmate-leaved **trumpet tree** or **cecropia** (*Cecropia obtusifolia*; A, 22) is very noticeable. Its branches grow in tiers and the leaves never form a closed canopy. With it often grows the weedy medium-sized **gunpowder tree** (*Trema orientalis*; A, 73), easily recognized at a distance because of the simple, alternate, toothed leaves that grow in a plane

king palm

trumpet tree

trumpet tree flowers

gunpowder tree

bingabing

bingabing flowers

down either side of the branch. The leaves are asymmetrical at the base and have 3 nearly equal longitudinal veins. Foliage and branches of gunpowder tree are covered with sticky hairs that make it unpleasant (but harmless) to touch. Trumpet and gunpowder trees shade lower vegetation along roadsides especially around the Hilo Airport and along Stainback Highway. One of the understory trees of this area, as well as a few places on O'ahu, is the peculiar Philippine **bingabing** (*Macaranga mappa*; A, 35). It has huge umbrella-like leaves, a giant version of those of the related macaranga (Section IV). The unusual red chenille-like flowers are hidden beneath the huge leaves.

REFORESTATION TREES

By the end of the 19th Century, Hawai'i's lowland forests were in such bad condition that serious efforts at reforestation, usually with alien trees, were undertaken. After a devastating fire near Hilo in 1928, several kinds of rapidly growing trees were seeded from airplanes. One of these, **melochia** (*Melochia umbellata*; F, 71), is now abundant in the area. It is a small tree with medium-sized heart-shaped leaves and small pink flowers. It is also found in a few places on Kaua'i and O'ahu. Probably the most important low-

melochia

Moluccan albizia

Grove of **Moluccan albizia**. Manoa Valley, O'ahu.

land reforestation tree on Kaua'i and O'ahu is **Moluccan albizia** (*Paraserianthes falcataria*; F, 36), a tall, spreading, flat-topped tree that does well in wet habitats. It is usually just called "albizia" in Hawai'i. This is the tree that fills the deep ravines near Wahiawa on O'ahu and arches over the highway in Kalihiwai Valley, Kaua'i. Hurricane Iniki in 1992 completely destroyed this beautiful tree arch, but so fast-growing is albizia that it will soon reach its former glory. Albizia spreads easily by its own seeds into open areas but is not considered a weed. Like many members of the pea family, albizia and the next species have white shaving-brush flowers and feathery, twice-compound leaves. Dense

black-wattle acacia

blackwood acacia

Formosan koa

columnar araucaria

thickets of **black-wattle acacia** (*Acacia mearnsii*; A, 36) grow in ravines and pastures around Kula, Maui, as well as a few places on Oʻahu and Hawaiʻi and at Kokeʻe, Kauaʻi. It was originally introduced for reforestation but has become a pest. Black-wattle is easily recognized by its feathery twice-compound leaves and densely crowded greenish young trunks. Its fuzzy pods are constricted between the seeds. Also belonging to the pea family, but with rather different leaves, is **blackwood acacia** (*Acacia melanoxylon*; F, 36). An Australian tree closely related to native koa (Sections VI and VII), it also has "false leaves" called phyllodes that are simple, elongated single blades, and more typical feathery acacia leaves on saplings. Its phyllodes are straighter than those of native koa. Blackwood acacia is widespread in disturbed places and has spread rapidly into areas of former native forest around Kokeʻe that lost their canopy in Hurricane Iniki. **Formosan koa**

(*Acacia confusa*; F, 36) is less wide-spread and lacks the feathery leaves on young trees. Its phyllodes are straigher and narrower and its pods are shorter than those of blackwood acacia and flat rather than curled. Look for it along the Tantalus/Round Top loop in Honolulu. Better known as an ornamental than as a forestry tree is **columnar araucaria** or **Cook pine** (*Araucaria columnaris*; F, G1), which, through a long chain of errors, has come to be known incorrectly as Norfolk Island pine, a different species entirely. This species comes from New Caledonia, but was misidentified in Hawai'i as the Norfolk Island tree, and Hawaiian trees then became the ancestors of virtually all the "Norfolk Island pines" growing in living rooms and bank lobbies nationwide. For a while, both species were listed as growing in Hawai'i, but it now appears that only this one is present. A particularly fine stand shades Lana'i City.

ORNAMENTAL SHRUBS AND VINES

Many plants with beautiful flowers or foliage enliven the understory of Hawai'i's secondary forest. **Pothos vine** (*Epipremnum pinnatum*; A, 79), which festoons trees on all islands, is familiar to most as a houseplant under the inaccurate

Trees festooned with **pothos vine.** Nu'uanu Valley, O'ahu.

pothos vine

pikake honohono

white shrimp plant

red hibiscus

Turk's cap

name "philodendron." Its heart-shaped leaves are often spangled with pale yellow spots. In very wet areas such as Nu'uanu Valley on O'ahu, a dense drapery of pothos vine often shades wild stands of **clerodendrum** or **pikake hono-hono** (*Clerodendrum philippinum*; A, 75) a popular ornamental shrub with fragrant pink-and-purple flowers. In this same area, as well as on Kaua'i and Hawai'i, the **white shrimp plant** (*Justicia betonica*; A, 1) has recently become a conspicuous roadside shrub. Its vertical spikes of white bracts that nearly hide the tiny lavender flowers are very distinctive. Many people assume that the ubiquitous **red hibiscus** (*Hibiscus rosa-sinensis*; A, 44), often thought of as the symbol of Hawai'i, is a native plant. Actually, most of the domestic hibiscus in Hawai'i, whether red or yellow (see Appendix 1), are horticultural hybrids or varieties of this non-native species. The various native red-flowered hibiscus (Section VI) are today very rare in the wild. Domestic red hibiscus is sparingly naturalized along roadsides but most of those seen are survivors of abandoned gardens. The same can be said of the related **Turk's cap** (*Malvaviscus penduliflorus*; A, 44) which looks like a red hibiscus whose hanging flowers remain closed. Another attractive garden escape is pink-flowered **rose myrtle** (*Rhodomyrtus tomentosa*; A, 51), present on all islands but especially common in the windward lowlands of Kaua'i. Its leaves resemble those of melastomes (see below), but are thicker, almost leathery.

Melastomes (Melastomaceae) are characterized by simple leaves with multiple prominent longitudinal veins (the lateral ones almost as large as the midrib). Many also have strong cross-veins that give the leaf surface a checkerboard look. Many melastomes with showy flowers prized as ornamentals are naturalized in Hawai'i. One of the most conspicuous, the purple-flowered tibouchina, grows at higher elevations and is discussed in the next section. **Pink melastome** (*Melastoma candidum*; A, 45), also called Indian rhododendron, has spread from cultivation on Kaua'i and Hawai'i. It is a shrub with rose-pink medium-sized 5-petaled flowers. Another melastome, whose flowers are smaller and white, is **tetrazygia**, native to southern Florida and the northern West Indies where it is known misleadingly as "wild guava." It is spreading from cultivation mostly along roadsides and in secondary rainforest around Hilo. Two melastomes are noteworthy because of the serious danger they pose to Hawai'i's native ecosystems. One of Hawai'i's most invasive and difficult to control rainforest weeds is **Koster's curse** or **clidemia** (*Clidemia hirta*; A, 45). On

rose myrtle

pink melastome

tetrazygia

clidemia

O'ahu, where it is widespread, it has made many mountain hiking trails unusable. It spreads rapidly into any clearing or opening in the canopy, preventing regeneration of native trees. On the neighbor islands, it is a more recent arrival and not yet a pest, but without control measures it is sure to become one. Clidemia is easily recognized by its rough-surfaced, typical melastome leaves, small white flowers, and hairy, dark blue, half-inch oval fruits. One of the most serious threats to Hawaii's ecosystems is **velvet leaf** or **purple plague** (*Miconia calvescens*; A, 45). It is an interesting-looking plant with huge melastome leaves that are purple underneath, but it should NEVER be cultivated in Hawai'i. In Tahiti, where in just a quarter-century *Miconia* has almost completely displaced natural ecosystems from sea level to mountaintop, it is called "green cancer." It crowds out almost all other plants; native animals cannot live in it. If you find velvet leaf growing in Hawai'i, destroy it if you can or call the Pest and Weed Control Specialists at the nearest office of the State Department of Agriculture.

velvet-leaf

VI. TEMPERATE MIXED FOREST

View from Mohihi Road, Koke'eState Park, Kaua'i.

FORESTS AT MIDDLE ELEVATIONS WITH MODERATE RAINFALL ARE THE RICHEST IN SPECIES IN THE HAWAIIAN ISLANDS, EVEN RICHER THAN NATIVE RAINFORESTS. MANY OF THE NATIVE PLANTS ARE NOW ENDANGERED SPECIES, DISPLACED BY ALIEN WEEDY SPECIES OR PLANTS PURPOSELY INTRODUCED FOR ONE REASON OR ANOTHER. BOTANISTS CALL IT "MIXED MESIC FOREST." ACCESSIBLE EXAMPLES OF THIS HABITAT ARE FOUND ON THE BIG ISLAND AROUND VOLCANO VILLAGE AND IN KIPUKA PUAULU IN HAWAII VOLCANOES NATIONAL PARK, ON KAUA'I AT KOKE'E STATE PARK, AND SEVERAL PLACES ABOVE HONOLULU ON O'AHU INCLUDING MT. TANTALUS. THESE VARIOUS COMMUNITIES ARE BY NO MEANS IDENTICAL, BUT ALL HAVE MODERATE TEMPERATURE AND RAINFALL AND THEY SHARE MANY SPECIES. DETERMINING THE BOUNDARIES OF THIS COMMUNITY IS DIFFICULT BECAUSE IT BLENDS IMPERCEPTABLY WITH DISTURBED DRY HABITATS AND SECONDARY RAINFOREST ON ONE HAND, AND NATIVE RAINFOREST ON THE OTHER. UNFORTUNATELY FOR THE REMAINING NATIVE ECOSYSTEMS, THAT MAKES MIXED TEMPERATE FOREST THE PERFECT CONDUIT FOR A GREAT MANY INVASIVE WEEDS.

Canopy of **'ōhi'a**.

Giant **koa** in full bloom

common soapberry

Native Trees and Shrubs

Though much altered, mid-elevation forest is still dominated by the same two canopy trees that shade the rainforest (Section VII), **'ōhi'a-lehua** (*Metrosideros polymorpha*; E, 51), with its gnarled trunks, peeling bark, and red shaving-brush flowers, and the towering **koa** (*Acacia koa*; E, 36), a magnificent tree with smooth gray bark and sickle-shaped leaves. Both trees are discussed in more detail in Section VII. **Common soapberry** (*Sapindus saponaria*; I, 68), with 2 Hawaiian names, **a'e** around Volcano and **manele** in Kona, is a dominant canopy tree in temperate mixed forest on the Big Island. The compound leaves, unusual among native trees, and distinctive fruit clusters easily distinguish it. Despite its oddly restricted Hawaiian range, this soapberry is not endemic because the same species also occurs on other Pacific islands as well as in Africa and tropical America.

Growing under the canopy are a host of smaller native trees and shrubs, so many as to be rather bewildering to the beginner. One way to sort them out is to notice the leaf arrangement: opposite, alternate, or whorled (3-5 leaves at a single node). Many are known under a single Hawaiian name, but are actually complexes of several species. An example is **kopiko** (*Psychotria* spp.; E, 65). Kopiko has opposite, simple, rather stiff shiny leaves, small white flowers, and orange fruits. The flowers and fruits are borne in clusters at the ends of branches rather than along the branch like those of pilo (*Coprosma* spp., Sections VII, IX), with which they might be confused, or coffee (Section V) to which kopiko is related. Much larger opposite leaves characterize the **Hawaiian olive** or **olopua** (*Nestegis sandwicensis*; E, 53), which can be observed in Kipuka Puaulu and at Koke'e. The leaves are very dark green and glossy, with a prominent bright yellow midrib. The fruits are indeed olive-like. At Koke'e only, look for **uahiapele** (*Melicope barbigera*; E, 66) a Kaua'i endemic that also has dark green, opposite, simple leaves. Both the scientific ("bearded") and Hawaiian ("Pele's smoke") names refer to the tree's most distinctive feature, a white fuzz along the midrib on the underside of the leaf. Another opposite-leaved small tree, this one with red midribs on paler yellow-green leaves, is **'ahakea** (*Bobea brevipes*; E, 65) found only on Kaua'i and O'ahu. Do not

kopiko

olopua

'ahakea

uahiapele

'āla'a

hao

confuse it with olomea (Section VII), a rainforest tree with opposite, sawtooth-edged leaves that also have red midribs. A tree whose leaves grow in a spiral pattern that makes them appear both opposite and alternate on the same tree is **'āla'a** (*Pouteria sandwicensis*; E, 69). Its milky sap was used in ancient Hawai'i as birdlime, the bird equivalent of flypaper. The leaves are usually leathery, larger than those of kopiko (Section VI), and the young ones are characteristically rust-colored especially underneath. 'Āla'a is found on all islands but is particularly noticeable around Koke'e. Another tree with milky sap is **hao** (*Rauvolfia sandwicensis*; E, 5), a small tree with pale bark and whorled leaves. The leathery leaves are very distinctive, long and narrow with closely spaced, nearly parallel side veins. The tiny white flowers are borne in clusters and mature into 1-inch purple-black soft fruits. Hao is found on all islands in a variety of habitats, even including dry forest (Section VIII) on the Big Island.

Alternate simple leaves characterize many trees of the mixed forest. Glossy dark green ones with smooth edges are found on several species of **pāpala** (*Charpentiera* spp.; E, 3). The most distinctive feature of all pàpala are the tiny red flowers in long dangling strings. The one shown (C. *obovata*)

pāpala

is found on all islands and is common in Kipuka Puaulu. Leaves with a similar color and texture but very different shape (shorter, rounder, and often with toothed edges) can be seen on **po'olā** (*Claoxylon sandwicense*; E, 35). It is a small tree of dry to mixed forest, fairly common on Kaua'i and O'ahu, rare and localized on the other islands. Paler green, long-pointed leaves are found on **kauila** (*Alphitonia ponderosa*; E, 62), a rare tree except on Kaua'i. Terminal leaf buds and leaf stems are rust-colored, but the leaves are thinner than those of the opposite-leaved ala'a (above). The 1-inch fruits are round with a ridge around the middle. Restricted to Kaua'i and O'ahu is **kālia** (*Elaeocarpus bifidus*; E, 32), a medium-sized tree whose thin, oval, pointed leaves have scalloped edges and asymmetrical bases. The true flowers are greenish white and borne in tight clusters at the leaf bases. However, nearly every tree harbors a mite that attacks the flowers and causes them to grow into a bright red gall or "witches broom" that looks like an inflorescence but has no discernible individual flowers. The mite is apparently a natural phenomenon and the trees are still able to reproduce. Kalia is conspicuous along trails in the Koke'e area. Often growing with it but less common is **Freycinet sandalwood** or **'ili'ahi**

po'olā

kauila

kālia with normal flowers

"False flowers" of **kālia**

Freycinet sandalwood

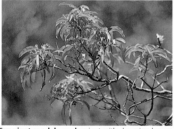

Freycinet sandalwood variant with drooping leaves

hō'awa

(*Santalum freycinetianum*; E, 67). During the early trade in fragrant sandalwood, these small trees nearly disappeared from Hawai'i but have made something of a comeback. Sandalwoods in general are best identified by their distinctive flowers and fruits. Sandalwood taxonomy is rather bewildering for the layman, and often very different-looking trees may belong to the same species. This one is found on all islands except Hawai'i, and is the most likely one to be found in wet forest. The leaves can be either stiff and upright or lax and drooping. Long, narrow leaves with rough upper surfaces characterize the various species of **ho'awa** (*Pittosporum* spp., E, 58), small trees with very distinctive seed capsules that split open to reveal a bright orange lining and sticky black seeds. The leaves are often so crowded at the ends of branches that their alternate arrangement is not obvious. The various species differ in flower color, degree of leaf roughness, and surface texture of fruit capsules. The example shown here is *P. hosmeri*, photographed in cultivation on Hawai'i. A closely related Big Island species (*P. hawaiiense*) has knobby rather than smooth capsules. Other species are found in rainforest on Kaua'i (Section VII).

Although the hibiscus most often seen in Hawai'i are alien, Hawai'i has an array of beautiful

Hawaiian red hibiscus

native species that are now quite rare. They are important horticulturally because they have contributed genes to many domestic hybrids. The native red hibiscus **koki'o 'ula** (Hibiscus kokio; E, 44) lives in scattered pockets in mixed forest on all islands but is much more likely to be seen in cultivation. More easily seen in the wild is the spectacular Kaua'i white hibiscus **koki'o kea** (Hibiscus waimeae; E, 44) which grows along Koke'e Road in the vicinity of Waimea Canyon. It is similar to the white hibiscus of O'ahu rainforests (next section) but is considered a Kaua'i endemic. In the same area as the white hibiscus grows another very unusual Kaua'i endemic, the **'iliau** (Wilkesia gymnoxyphium; E, 9). It looks like a shrub on a pole. Despite its appearance, it is a member of the daisy family and belongs to the

Kaua'i white hibiscus

'iliau

group that includes the various species of *Dubautia* and Maui's spectacular silversword (Section X). Like the latter, 'iliau grows for some years, then puts all its energy into an immense flowering stalk before it dies. 'Iliau can be easily seen along Koke'e Road near the intersection with Waimea Canyon Road. Be careful not to confuse nonblooming 'iliau with **Kaua'i halapepe** (*Pleomele aurea*; E, 78) which is usually found at somewhat higher elevation. Halapepe has a similar growth form, but it is a larger plant with longer, broader leaves that tend to droop. If you are fortunate, you may see the spectacular dangling golden flower cluster of halapepe.

FERNS

🍂 Mixed forest habitats on all islands support several shrubby or vining ferns. The most widespread is **Pacific false staghorn** or **'uluhe** (**I** *Dicranopteris linearis*; I, F7), which is also prominent in secondary forest down to sea level as well as rainforest openings. It is also native to other islands throughout the tropical Pacific. 'Uluhe quickly invades bare areas such as road cuts, landslides on steep cliffs, and tree falls in wet areas. The viny stems zigzag and branch at each joint, allowing 'uluhe to nearly tie itself in knots. This unusual growth pattern produces

Kaua'i halapepe

'uluhe 1

'uluhe 2

very dense, almost impenetrable tangles. Huge areas in secondary rainforest and temperate mixed forest in Hawai'i are covered with 'uluhe. Less common is an endemic **'uluhe** (**2** *Sticherus owyhensis*; E, F7), which differs in its larger fronds with "leaflets" that continue along the entire stem with no gaps except at the very base. The closely related **giant false staghorn** or **'uluhe lau nui** (*Diplopterygium pinnatum*; I, F7) grows with 'uluhe in cooler areas but is much less common. It has larger fronds up to 2 feet long that branch only once or twice on a stem. All 3 species can be seen together on the Alaka'i Swamp Trail on Kaua'i. Also large and shrubby, but not forming dense thickets is the **bracken fern** or **kilau** (*Pteridium aquilinum*; I, F4), a fern of semi-open forest floor. Bracken is found worldwide, its spores spreading easily on the wind. It is distinguished by its triple-compound fronds, the first division of which produces two side branches that grow in a different plane from the main frond. Among the bracken,

'uluhe lau nui

bracken fern/kilau

Christmas-tree clubmoss/wawae 'iole

as well as forming tangles amidst 'uluhe, is a fern relative called **Christmastree clubmoss** or **wawae 'iole** (*Lycopodiella cernua*; I, F8). The English name refers to the plant's resemblance to a miniature conifer, and the Hawaiian name to the resemblance of the dangling spore bodies to rats' feet. Hawai'i has several smaller species of clubmoss with upright spore cases.

FORESTRY TREES AND SHRUBS

Cooler upland forests in Hawai'i are even more heavily influenced by reforestation than the secondary rainforest. Indeed, in some places the original koa and 'ōhi'a canopy has been entirely replaced by purposely planted alien trees. Hawai'i's most frequently planted trees, both for reforestation and as ornamentals, are eucalypts. With a few exceptions, identifying the more than 30 species growing wild in the islands is a botanical nightmare, so it is often best just to call them all "eucalyptus." Eucalyptus typically have long narrow leaves, brushy white flowers, and an aroma of camphor, but there is wide variation among species. The most common is **swamp-mahogany** (*Eucalyptus robusta*; F, 51), a tall straight tree with characteristic deeply furrowed spongy bark. It is no longer planted by forestry officials, but huge old

swamp-mahogany

blue gum leaves and fruits

trees are still important as windbreaks on most islands. A particularly fine stand can be seen above Mountain View on the Hilo-Volcano highway. Large forests of swamp-mahogany along Koke'e Road on Kaua'i were particularly hard-hit by Hurricane Iniki. It remains to be seen whether these groves will regenerate or be replaced by more aggressive species. Australian **blue gum** (*Eucalyptus globulus*; F, 51) is a more typical eucalypt. It came to Hawai'i over a century ago and now is a prominent part of the landscape. Visitors to the crater of Haleakalā drive through grove after aromatic grove of planted blue gum, and it is one of the dominant trees along Tantalus Drive above downtown Honolulu. When in bloom, the Tantalus trees attract the endemic O'ahu 'Amakihi, a Hawaiian honey-

blue gum trunks

paperbark

Flowers, fruits, and foliage of **paperbark**.

Bagras eucalyptus

creeper. The third most often planted tree in Hawai'i is the distinctive **paperbark** or **cajeput tree** (*Melaleuca quinquenervia*; F, 51), a eucalyptus relative from Australia. The tree's most distinctive feature is its spongy, white, peeling bark but note also the simple leaves with several longitudinal veins, white "bottle-brush" flowers, and small woody fruit capsules. Huge stands of paperbark have been planted for watershed protection on several islands, and the tree has spread on its own into more diverse forests. Probably the most recognizable of the less common eucalypts is **Bagras eucalyptus** (*Eucalyptus deglupta*; F, 51), often called "rainbow eucalyptus" in Hawai'i, which comes from tropical islands north of Australia, including the Philippines. Its leaves resemble those of blue gum, but the trunk is smooth with multicolored patches where pieces have peeled away. It can be found on all islands but is not common in the wild. A nice grove is maintained at Keahua Arboretum on Kaua'i.

The New Zealand **karakanut** (*Corynocarpus laevigatus*; F, 28) is a small tree widely planted in Hawai'i but commonly naturalized only on Kaua'i. It was aerially seeded over the interior of that island, and is common around Koke'e State Park. It has leathery dark green leaves and 2-inch soft orange fruits. They are edible, though the seeds are poisonous, making this tree easily spread by feral pigs who deposit the undigested seeds with their own fertilizer. Another forestry tree that has become naturalized in some areas is **Australian toon** (*Toona ciliata*; F, 46) characterized by huge even-compound (i. e. lacking a terminal leaflet) leaves with up to 10 pairs of asymmetrical leaflets and dangling clusters of tiny white flowers. It has been widely planted around Hilo, and can be easily found on Tantalus Drive in Honolulu. The Tantalus area has, in fact, become a virtual botanical garden of trees introduced by state foresters. Among them, look for a tree with 3-part compound leaves. This is **koka** (B*ischofia javanica*; A, 35), rather recently planted by foresters but apparently naturalized. The only other trees with trifoliate leaves one is likely to see most places in Hawaii are the native olapa and lapalapa (Section VI).

ESCAPED ORNAMENTALS

🐾 The very odd-shaped leaves of **tree daisy** (*Montanoa hibiscifolia*; A, 9) are hard to miss on the Tantalus-Round Top loop above Honolulu. When the daisy-like white flowers are not present, one could easily mistake tree daisy for paper mulberry (Section V), whose young leaves have a similar trident shape. Older leaves of both plants may be heart-

karakanut

Australian toon

koka

Thicket of **tree daisy**.

tree daisy

night cestrum in bloom

night cestrum fruits

cup-of-gold

shaped. Tree daisy is also found in similar habitats on the neighbor islands except Moloka'i. Also established on Tantalus from garden plantings is **night cestrum** (*Cestrum nocturnum*; A, 70), whose tubular yellowish green flowers open at night to release a wonderfully sweet aroma. The half-inch fruits are smooth, white, and berrylike. Night cestrum also grows in the lowlands of Kaua'i. Its day-scented counterpart, day cestrum (C. *diurnum*; not shown), has white flowers and is naturalized on Kaua'i, O'ahu, and Moloka'i. Both cestrums originated in the West Indies and are widely planted in the tropics. In the same family and also a garden escape is the spectacular **cup-of-gold** (*Solandra maxima*; C, 70) vine, whose huge leathery yellow flowers look almost artificial. Cup-of-gold grows abundantly along the Tantalus-Round Top loop where it appears to be naturalized. One of the more unusual ornamentals that has spread into mixed forest is the **lipstick tree** or **'alaea** (*Bixa orellana*; A, 12). Its white or pink flowers even-

lipstick tree

fiddlewood

tually produce bright red spiny pods that open to reveal seeds covered with a bright red sticky substance that resembles lipstick. Its heart-shaped leaves resemble those of several other plants in the same habitat, but note the red main veins. Lipstick tree first gained a foothold in Nu'uanu Valley, O'ahu but is is now found also on Kaua'i, Moloka'i, and Maui. It is still very popular in Hawaiian gardens. The West Indian **fiddlewood** (*Citharexylum caudatum*; A, 75) has a similar history. It is a popular Honolulu ornamental that has become naturalized in the mountains behind the city. It has opposite simple leaves and terminal spikes of white flowers that mature into half-inch orange or black berrylike fruits.

Mexican elder

A fruit tree that was brought to Hawai'i more for its large sprays of white flowers than for its tiny purple berries is **Mexican elder** (*Sambucus mexicanus*; A, 18). Note its compound leaves with toothed leaflets. Look for Mexican elder in cool upland areas of Kaua'i, O'ahu, East Maui, and Hawai'i. A very com-

thimbleberry

Himalayan raspberry

pyracantha

mon understory plant in secondary forest on all the islands, especially along roads and trails, is **thimbleberry** (*Rubus rosifolius*; A, 64), more correctly called Mauritius raspberry. It has small white flowers and red fruits much smaller than the native 'ākala raspberry (Section VI).

Thimbleberries are quite edible and can be refreshing on a long hike, but they have little flavor and hardly make up for the annoyance of the plant's prickles. Recently, the **Himalayan raspberry** (*Rubus ellipticus*; A, 64), a related species with yellow fruits, has become established around Volcano Village on the Big Island. It is taller and more rambling than thimbleberry and has more vicious thorns. **Pyracantha** (*Pyracantha angustifolia*; A, 64) has also escaped from cultivation in the Volcano area as well as at Koke'e, Kaua'i. Its flowers look much like those of thimbleberry and blackberry (below), but its fruits look like rose hips and it has simple leaves. The casual observer could mistake pyracantha for several native species of pilo (*Coprosma* spp.).

blackberry

ALIEN INVADERS IN THE FOREST

🐌 The worst thorns of any "berry" are found on **blackberry** (*Rubus argutus*; A, 64) from the American southeast. Despite its tasty black fruit, blackberry is not a welcome addition to Hawai'i's flora. It is very aggressive, moving from open fields and roadsides into treefalls or burns in forests where it forms huge "briar patches" that prevent the regeneration of native plants. It is easily spread by birds, hikers, and feral pigs and is exceedingly difficult to control once established. Blackberry is a particularly serious weed on Kaua'i where it is taking advantage of the destruction of the forest canopy by Hurricane Iniki to move into new areas, but it is a threat to native forests on all islands.

A "beautiful weed" of Hawai'i's uplands is **glory-bush, lasiandra,** or **princess-flower** (*Tibouchina urvilleana*; A, 45). With its deep purple flowers, pink buds, and red leaves scattered among the green, this tall shrub is hard to miss. It is the most conspicuous roadside plant in Volcano Village and Koke'e State Park and is also found on O'ahu and Maui. As with many other introduced plants, glory-bush crowds out more interesting native shrubs. Perhaps the most serious ecological threat among the "flowers gone wild" in Hawai'i is **banana poka** (*Passiflora mollissima*; A, 55). This

glory-bush or **lasiandra**

banana poka

Hanging fruit of **banana poka**

strawberry guava

Flowers of **strawberry guava**

high-climbing vine is a kind of passionfruit, but its disparaging local name ("poka" means "offal") shows that Hawaiians never liked it. Feral pigs love the banana-shaped fruits, and have spread this weed deep into rainforests on Kaua'i and Hawai'i. But it is an ill wind that blows no good, and some native honeycreepers, such as the scarlet 'I'iwi, feed readily on the nectar of the dangling pink blossoms.

We do not normally think of fruit trees as weeds, but that designation is certainly appropriate for **strawberry guava** (*Psidium cattleianum*; A, 51), a relative of common guava (Section III) that grows at higher elevations. It has smaller shiny leaves, smooth bark with peeling patches, and much smaller fruits with red edible rind that tastes vaguely of strawberry. Pigs and introduced birds love it, and therein lies much of the problem. Strawberry guava is a small tree that can grow in very tight thickets with trunks only inches apart. They are impossible to

walk through and the trees produce soil chemicals that inhibit the growth of other plants. Some roads and trails between Volcano Village and Hilo on the Big Island and in Koke'e State Park on Kaua'i are virtually walled in by strawberry guava. These same areas are the epicenter of infestation by another pest, the **firetree** (*Myrica faya*; A, 49). Native to the Azores, firetree apparently came to Hawai'i with Portuguese immigrants who made a wine from its black fruits. It presents all of the same problems as strawberry guava, growing in uniform stands that crowd out everything else. With glory-bush, banana poka, strawberry guava, firetree, blackberry, and clidemia already displacing huge tracts of forest, and velvet-leaf poised to strike, Hawai'i's native forests are in serious jeopardy.

In a category all its own is **marijuana** or **pakalolo** (*Cannabis sativa*; C, 17). Whether it is naturalized in Hawai'i is problematical, but it is certainly widely cultivated, usually in small plots hidden in mixed forest

firetree

(formerly in now-disappearing cane-fields). A hiker who comes upon such a plot is in grave danger, not from the plants but from either armed guards or booby traps. One would do well to learn to recognize pakalolo! This illegal plant is sometimes said to be Hawai'i's top cash crop.

Typical vegetative growth of **firetree**.

marijuana/pakalolo

VII. NATIVE RAINFOREST

View of Lana'i from rainforest of Kamakou Preserve, Moloka'i.

WHEN MOST PEOPLE THINK OF RAINFOREST, THEY VISUALIZE A TARZAN-LIKE JUNGLE OF MULTILAYERED TREES DRAPED WITH LIANAS. ACTUALLY, THE TERM APPLIES TO ANY FOREST THAT RECEIVES SUFFICIENT RAINFALL, FROM THE TEMPERATE CONIFEROUS FORESTS OF THE PACIFIC NORTHWEST TO THE CLASSIC BROADLEAVED FORESTS OF THE AMAZON BASIN. HAWAIIAN RAINFORESTS ARE SO DISTINCTIVE THAT MANY OF THE GENERALIZATIONS ABOUT THIS LIFE ZONE GIVEN IN ECOLOGY TEXTBOOKS DO NOT APPLY. CONTINENTAL TROPICAL RAINFORESTS ARE NOTED FOR THEIR HUGE NUMBERS OF PLANT AND ANIMAL SPECIES. BECAUSE THEY GROW ON THE WORLD'S MOST ISOLATED ARCHIPELAGO, HAWAIIAN RAIN-FORESTS ARE ACTUALLY SPECIES POOR. ONLY A FEW ANCESTRAL PLANTS COULD SURVIVE THE OCEAN CROSSING TO COLONIZE THE ISLANDS. AS A RESULT, THE FOREST CANOPY IN

MOST PLACES IS FORMED BY ONLY ONE OR TWO SPECIES ('ŌHI'A AND KOA). ON CONTINENTS, RAINFORESTS ARE OFTEN CALLED "GALLERY FORESTS" IN REFERENCE TO THE MULTISTORIED PATTERN OF TREE GROWTH. IN HAWAI'I, RAINFORESTS HAVE ONLY 3 DEFINABLE STORIES: CANOPY, UNDERSTORY, AND GROUND LEVEL. LIKE THE CANOPY, THE OTHER 2 LAYERS MAY HAVE ONLY A FEW SPECIES IN A GIVEN AREA. ALTHOUGH RICH IN EPIPHYTES (PLANTS THAT GROW ON OTHER PLANTS FOR SUPPORT BUT DO NOT TAKE NOURISHMENT FROM THEM) AND SMALLER VINES, THESE FORESTS HAVE RELATIVELY FEW LARGE LIANAS. INDEED, HAWAIIAN RAINFOREST ACTUALLY HAS FEWER NATIVE PLANT SPECIES THAN TEMPERATE MIXED FOREST (SECTION VI).

BUT BY ITS VERY UNIQUENESS, HAWAIIAN NATIVE RAINFOREST IS A MAGNIFICENT RESOURCE FOR SCIENTIFIC STUDY AS WELL AS THE MAIN WATERSHED FOR THE ISLANDS. WITHOUT IT, NEITHER SUGAR NOR THE CITY OF HONOLULU COULD HAVE GROWN IN HAWAI'I. PRESERVATION OF THE REMAINING RAINFOREST IS CRITICAL TO THE LONG-TERM SURVIVAL OF HUMANS AS WELL AS ENDEMIC ORGANISMS. FORTUNATELY, FAIRLY LARGE TRACTS STILL REMAIN IN THE FEW ROADLESS AREAS SUCH AS KAUA'I'S ALAKAI PLATEAU, THE WINDWARD SLOPES OF HALEAKALĀ AND UPPER KIPAHULU VALLEY ON MAUI, HAKALAU FOREST NATIONAL WILDLIFE REFUGE, OLA'A TRACT AND PU'U MAKA'ALA NATURAL AREA RESERVE, AND KA'U FOREST RESERVE AMONG OTHERS ON HAWAI'I. A FEW AREAS, SUCH AS SOME SELDOM-VISITED KIPUKAS (POCKETS OF OLD FOREST SURROUNDED BY YOUNGER LAVA FLOWS) ON HAWAI'I, ARE STILL ALMOST WEED-FREE. IN GENERAL, VISITING THESE AREAS REQUIRES CONSIDERABLE EFFORT, BUT A FEW ROADS PROVIDE ACCESS TO NATIVE RAINFOREST. THE MOST ACCESSIBLE AREAS ARE REACHED VIA PIHEA AND ALAKAI SWAMP TRAILS ON KAUA'I, THROUGH NATURE CONSERVANCY TOURS OF WAIKAMOI PRESERVE ON MAUI, AND VIA THE SADDLE ROAD AND WRIGHT ROAD IN VOLCANO VILLAGE ON THE BIG ISLAND.

'ōhi'a-lehua

Mature fruits of **'ōhi'a-lehua**

Large buds of **'ōhi'a** variety *dieteri.*

lehua mamo

CANOPY TREES

🍃 True Hawaiian rainforest is always dominated by **'ōhi'a-lehua** (*Metrosideros polymorpha*; E, 51; "'òhi'a" refers to the tree only, "lehua" to the blossoms), which forms virtually the entire closed canopy. This remarkable tree may be a pioneer on a recent lava flow, a low shrub of montane bogs, a gnarled guardian of windswept ridges, or a tall, straight, tree suitable for construction. The scientific name *polymorpha,* "many forms," is certainly appropriate. Lehua blossoms lack petals; they are brush-like clusters of stamens and pistils growing from a calyx cup in which nectar collects. They are adapted for wind pollination, but in Hawai'i's rainforests the job is probably most often accomplished by native birds such as the 'Ākohekohe, which even has a "pollen brush" on its forehead. The flowers mature into hard woody capsules. Typical 'ōhi'a has bright red flowers and small buds, but the variety *dieteri*, found on Kaua'i, has unusually large reddish

lehua papa

buds. In the Ko'olau Mountains of O'ahu, look for the yellow flowers of **lehua mamo** (*Metrosideros macropus*; E, 51). It differs also in having longer narrower leaves with longer petioles (leaf stems). Another Ko'olau endemic is **lehua papa** (*Metrosideros rugosa*; E, 51), a low-growing species of high ridges. It has lumpy-looking, strongly convex silvery leaves.

koa

Piercing the 'ōhi'a canopy here and there and towering over the rainforest is the majestic **koa** (*Acacia koa*; E, 36). At the upper limits of the forest, where less rain falls, koa may be the dominant tree, almost forming a continuous canopy. The sickle-shaped apparent leaves of koa are actually modified petioles that botanists call phyllodes. Saplings have twice-compound feathery true leaves that reveal koa's relationship to locusts and acacias. Larger saplings may even have feathery leaves attached to expanded petioles. Koa flowers are smaller than lehua, but are also an important source of nectar. They are small, yellow, fuzzy balls without petals. Koa is much in demand by craftsmen for its beautiful reddish wood, and is finally being grown for that purpose (instead of alien trees) in a few places on the Big Island.

Two different foliage types of **koa**.

Only a few other trees reach the rainforest canopy. On all islands except Hawai'i grows a relative of 'ōhi'a-lehua called **'ōhi'a-hā** (*Syzygium sandwicensis*; E, 51)but the

'ōhi'a-hā

'ōhi'a-hā flowers

'ohe

'ohe kiko olā

loulu

relationship is by no means obvious. 'Ohi'a-hā has opposite, simple, smooth-edged leaves that tend to grow upwards. They are often concave with edges rolled under. They resemble leaves of several species of 'alani and kōlea (see below) but have distinctive red midribs. Flowers of 'ōhi'a-hā are very different from the shaving-brush flowers often seen in the myrtle family. They are green, with a round fleshy center and four inconspicuous petals. The red or pink half-inch fruits grow in clusters at the tips of branches. A further distinguishing feature of 'ōhi'a-hā is its reddish brown 4-angled young stems.

Very distinctive canopy trees with large, leathery, pinnately compound leaves, are the several species of **'ohe** (*Tetraplasandra* spp.). They vary in details of flowers and fruits, things best left to the experts, and are generally uncommon but very conspicuous among the small-leaved 'ōhi'as. 'Ohe grow on all islands with the typical one shown (*T. hawaiensis*; E, 7) found from Moloka'i to Hawai'i. Two closely related **'ohe kiko'ola** (*T. waialealae*, shown, and *T. waimeae*; E, 7), with very large fruits, are endemic to Kaua'i. They are conspicuous along trails leading from Koke'e into the Alaka'i area. The latter species has once-compound flower clusters and shorter, rounder fruits. Emerging above the canopy here and there in all Hawaiian rain-

loulu hiwa

forests are various species of fan palms called **loulu** (*Pritchardia* spp.; E, 80). Paleontological evidence shows that loulu was much more common in Hawai'i's ancient past. Today, they grow solitarily or in small scattered groves. The 19 or so species are tricky to identify, but all have fairly restricted ranges so locality is the most important thing to know. The example shown here (*P. beccariana*) can be found along the Big Island's Stainback Highway. A distinctive shorter species, **loulu hiwa** (*P. martii*; E, 80) lives on windswept ridges in the rainforest of O'ahu's Ko'olau Mountains.

hapu'u

LARGE FERNS

Prominent in the rainforest understory is **Hawaiian tree-fern** or **hapu'u** (*Cibotium glaucum*; E, F5). In

Young fiddleheads of **hapu'u**.

'ama'u

'ama'u

Wallich's woodfern

laukāhi nunui

Hawaii Volcanoes National Park, tree-ferns may form a secondary closed canopy beneath the 'ōhi'a trees. Usually, however, they are one of many smaller rainforest trees. The species shown here, characterized by rust-colored "fur" on the leaf bases, is the most common and widespread but several smaller species of more restricted distribution complicate matters. Just call them all hapu'u. An easier distinction is between hapu'u and the smaller tree-ferns called **'ama'u** (Sadleria spp. E, F3). 'Ama'u fronds are double-compound whereas those of hapu'u are triple-compound. Also, the young fronds are often tinged red or orange (see also Section X). As with hapu'u, the smaller tree-ferns are actually a complex of species that are difficult to tell apart, with one being common and widespread, the others more restricted. Rainforests also harbor some "miniature tree-ferns." An example is **Wallich's woodfern** (Dryopteris wallichiana; I, F1), whose circular crown of fronds make it look like a giant shuttlecock. It's "trunk" is only a few inches high, and grows from the ground or as an epiphyte. Another conspicuous, but very different looking, rainforest fern that can be either terrestrial or epiphytic is **stag's tongue** or **laukāhi nunui** (Elaphoglossum aemulum; E, F6). Its fronds are a single undivided blade, and clumps of them often form huge "skirts" around the trunks of large trees.

UNDERSTORY TREES AND SHRUBS

◗ Beneath the rainforest canopy grow two trees that seem particularly common and noticeable because of their trifoliate compound leaves and clusters of dull purple fruits. (The mainland rhyme about "leaves of 3" does not apply in Hawai'i.) **'Ōlapa** (*Cheirodendron trigynum*; E, 7) is found throughout Hawaiian rainforests and is characterized by tooth-edged leaflets longer than they are wide. The species shown is the most common even on Kaua'i, but that island also has 3 other species of 'ōlapa, all with restricted distributions and differences in leaves or fruits. The related **lapalapa** (*Cheirodendron platyphyllum*; E, 7), restricted to Kaua'i and O'ahu, has yellow-green leaflets broader than long that tremble in the slightest breeze, imparting a slight resemblance to aspens. The name is imitative of the sound made by the back-and-forth motion, which is said to have also inspired the swaying motions of the hula.

Several other understory trees are easily identified by their foliage. **Olomea** (*Perrottetia sandwicensis*; E, 23) is especially common on Kaua'i but is found in all Hawaiian rainforests. It has simple, alternate yellow-green leaves with saw-toothed edges and prominent veins that are depressed into the upper surface. Most distinc-

'ōlapa

lapalapa

olomea

ho'awa

ha'iwale

kanawao flowers

kanawao fruits

tive are the bright red petioles, midribs, and lateral veins. Equally distinctive is a species of **ho'awa** (*Pittosporum gayanum*; E, 58) endemic to the rainforests of Kaua'i. It has long rough-surfaced leaves with a very prominent network of veins. Its white flowers bloom in clusters along the main branches below the leaves, and its nutlike fruits have a rough, wrinkled surface like that of the leaves. Kaua'i's Alaka'i region also has a distinctive species of **ha'iwale** (*Cyrtandra longifolia*; E, 38) a small tree that can be seen on trails around Koke'e but is more common deeper in the rainforest. The glossy pale green leaves have prominent curved lateral veins sunken into the surface. The slightly curved trumpet-shaped white flowers bloom below the leaves and the fruits resemble shiny, 1-inch elongated eggs. An immediately recognizable and common shrub of Hawaiian rainforests is **kanawao** (*Broussaisia arguta*; E, 40). The strongly curving lateral veins and pale "teeth" along the edge make its leaves unique. It bears an apical cluster of variously colored flowers that mature into fleshy red to deep maroon fruits. Alternate, dark green, leathery leaves characterize **Hawaiian holly** or **kāwa'u** (*Ilex anomala*; E, 6). They are easily distinguished from other simple leaves by their oval shape and net-like vein pattern impressed into the upper leaf surface. Kàwa'u has small white

kāwa'u

alani

flowers that produce shiny black fruits among the leaf clusters.

Several rainforest understory trees have opposite simple leaves with smooth edges. The nearly 50 species of **alani** (Melicope spp.; E, 66; until recently placed in the genus Pelea) have opposite or whorled oval or oblong leaves and four-parted fruits. The species shown (M. *clusiifolia*) is one of the more easily recognized and widespread species with its thick leathery leaves and green fruits that form along the stem where leaves have fallen. The leaves will remind those familiar with the Appalachian Mountains of rhododendron. Another easily identifiable member of the genus is the Kaua'i endemic **mokihana** (Melicope anisata; E, 66) all parts of which have a strong anise scent. Its leaves are smaller than those of most species of alani, many of which also smell at least faintly of anise. Mokihana has tiny green vase-shaped flowers that produce yellow-green 4-parted fruits. It is the traditional lei plant of Kaua'i, but care must be taken with

mokihana

kōlea lau nui

Mature fruits of **kōlea lau nui**.

pilo kea

pilo 1

pilo 2

its use because the aromatic sap is a skin irritant. Thick leaves with prominent contrastingly colored midribs are also found on **kōlea lau nui** (*Myrsine lessertiana*; E, 50) whose most distinctive feature is brightly colored terminal leaves that may be yellow, pink, or pale purple. The small reddish flowers and quarter-inch, shiny, black, cherrylike fruits form densely along bare areas on the branches below the leaf clusters. A variety of small-leaved species of *Myrsine*, collectively called kōlea, also grow in Hawaiian forests. All have opposite simple leaves and purple to black fruits. Some of the largest opposite simple leaves are found on **pilo kea** (*Platydesma spathulata*; E, 66) a small tree of rainforests on the 4 largest islands. Its leaves may be half a meter long but usually are smaller, thick and leathery, with the edges rolled under. At the leaf bases grow bell-shaped flowers with 4 white petals and 4-parted globular 1-inch fruits.

Several rainforest shrubs have conspicuous red or orange soft fruits. The most common belong to a group of species called **pilo** (*Coprosma* spp.; E, 65), which have one-seeded half-inch fruits that show the relationship to coffee (Section V). The fruits are borne along the branch at the leaf bases rather than in a cluster at the end as in kopiko (Section VI), another coffee relative. Pilos have opposite, simple, smooth-edged, relatively thin leaves that vary widely in size. One of the most common species (**1** C. *ochracea*) is found on all islands except Kaua'i, where it is replaced by the related C. *kauensis*. Around Hawaii Volcanoes National Park grows a distinctive species (**2** C. *rhynchocarpa*) identified by the short "beak" on its fruits. Another distinctive pilo, better known as **'ōlena** (C. *waimeae*; E, 65), is endemic to Kaua'i. It has unusual male flowers with long dangling stamens. The female flowers are more conventional and the fruits are orange. Dangling deep red (usually) berries are found on a wet-forest species of **Hawaiian huckleberry** or **'ōhelo** (*Vaccinium dentatum*; E, 34). It is a low-growing shrub usually found in edges and openings in rainforest, often as an epiphyte. Its flowers are tubular, white to green with red or purple stripes outside. This species can be distinguished from the more familiar 'ōhelo that grows on lava flows (Section X) and in subalpine scrub (Section IX) by its smaller, darker fruits and narrower, longer leaves that are always saw-toothed along the edge. Rainforests also have a larger *Vaccinium* called **tree ohelo** or **'ōhelo kau la'au** (V. *calycinum*; E, 34). It has larger leaves than other 'ōhelo that tend to be broader toward the distal end. Its fruits are always bright carmine red. All 'ōhelo berries are quite edible, though

'ōlena male flowers

'ōlena

'ōhelo

'ōhelo kau la'au

'ākala

'ākala flowers

'ākala prickles

māmaki

often insipid, with many tiny seeds rather than one large one. These 2 species are found on all islands that have rainforest. The largest edible fruit in Hawaiian rainforests is **Hawaiian raspberry** or **'ākala** (*Rubus hawaiensis*; E, 64), which grows on Kaua'i, Moloka'i, Maui, and Hawai'i. The large size of the berries, which are occasionally yellow, and the magenta flower color distinguish this native species from similar introduced fruits (Section VI). 'Ākala is sometimes cited as an example of the loss of defenses in island plants, but even though it lacks large thorns, the stems are covered with sharp bristles that can be very unpleasant to grasp, as many a hiker can attest. The plants may form dense stands in forest openings and along trails. 'Ākala berries are rather sour, but can be made into tasty pies and jams.

Other Shrubs

🐾 A native shrub that is a better example of the loss of defenses is **māmaki** (*Pipturus albidus*; E, 74), a shrubby nettle that lacks the stinging hairs of other members of that family. It usually has rather papery leaves with three prominent longitudinal veins that may be tinged red. The leaves are eaten by caterpillars of the Kāmehameha butterfly (*Vanessa tameiameiae*). Māmaki flowers are inconspicuous, and the fruits are unusual white masses with the seeds borne on the surface, somewhat in the manner of a strawberry. This species is found on all islands, but 3 other mamaki species have very restricted distributions on Maui and Kaua'i.

An important phenomenon in the evolution of all Hawaiian plants and animals is adaptive radiation. By this process, a single ancestral colonizing species gives rise to a group of species that fill a variety of roles in the natural community different from that of the founder. Rainforests are home to one of the more famous examples, the lobelioids. They are so named because the founder species belonged to the genus *Lobelia*, which includes many continental wildflowers with straight, tubular, purple flowers. The several native species still in that genus have become woody "rosette plants" (i. e. a circle of leaves on the end of a tall stem like a palm) and the flowers have developed curved corollas that fit the beaks of native honeycreepers. Like **Hillebrand's lobelia** (*Lobelia hillebrandii*; E, 16) of East Maui, they are mostly rare plants with restricted distribution. From *Lobelia* evolved several other shrubby genera. Some members of the genus *Cyanea*, such as **hāhā-lua** (*C. leptostegia*; E, 16) which grows along trails in the Koke'e area, retain the rosette growth form. But among

Hillebrand's lobelia

hāhā-lua

Branching growth form of **hāhā**.

hāhā

Kaua'i koli'i rosette growth form

Kaua'i koli'i flower close-up

hāhā'aiakamanu

hāhā'aiakamanu fruit

the dozens of *Cyanea* species are some that have branched trunks, as in a species of **hāhā** (C. *angustifolia*; E, 16) that is common along O'ahu's Aiea Trail. Also a rosette plant is the spectacular **Kaua'i koli'i** (*Trematolobelia kauaiensis*; E, 16) which grows along the Pihea Trail and has related species on other islands. It differs in bearing its cerise flowers on a radial spray of horizontal branches rather than a single vertical spike. The most divergent rainforest species are in the genus *Clermontia*, with many-branched trunks like typical shrubs. The genus includes more than 20 species that go under the collective name 'ōhā. **Hāhā'aiakamanu** (C. *fauriei*; E, 16), whose name refers to the fact that its nectar is favored by native honeycreepers, is the only species on Kaua'i. Around Thurston Lava Tube in Hawaii Volcanoes National Park and elsewhere on the Big Island, another **'ōhā** (C. *parviflora*; E, 16) can be seen.

Another example of adaptive radiation has as its founder the common beach naupaka (Section I).

'ōhā

From this indigenous coastal plant have evolved several montane species of rather different appearance, but all with the asymmetrical "half-flowers" characteristic of the genus. Several species are called **naupaka kuahiwi** (*Scaevola* spp.; E, 39) and have long narrow leaves that may be coarsely toothed along the distal edge, white or pale flowers, and black fruits. The ones shown here (**1** S. *gaudichaudiana* of Kaua'i and O'ahu; **2** S. *procera* of Kaua'i and Moloka'i) are typical. Kaua'i and O'ahu are also home to **'ohe naupaka** (*Scaevola glabra*; E, 39), with similar foliage but very different curved tubular yellow flowers. Close examination of the distal end of the flower shows its similarity to those of other *Scaevola*.

Adaptive radiation has also produced several rainforest members of the mostly dry-country group that includes the famous silversword (Section X), 'iliau (Section VI), and the various members of the genus *Dubautia* (Sections IX and X). One rainforest **na'ena'e** (**1** *Dubautia*

naupaka kuahiwi 1

naupaka kuahiwi 2

'ohe naupaka

na'ena'e 1

na'ena'e 2

na'ena'e 'ula

O'ahu white hibiscus

manono flowers

manono ripe fruits

reticulata; E, 9) shown here is from East Maui. Its leaves and flowers resemble those of its subalpine relatives but it is a small tree with many intertwining branches. Another species (**2** D. *plantaginea*) is found in all Hawaiian rainforests. It has large, rather fleshy, somewhat drooping leaves and purple flowers. It is imtermediate between the dryland species and the following. On Kaua'i, the very distinctive endemic **na'ena'e ula** (*Dubautia railliardioides*; E, 9) has purple flower stems, white flowers, long drooping leaves often purple-tinged at base, and viny twisting trunks.

Some components of the rainforest shrub layer are so distinctive that they cannot be easily grouped. One of Hawai'i's most spectacular native flowers is **O'ahu white hibiscus** or **koki'o ke'oke'o** (*Hibiscus arnottianus*; E, 44) which can be found along many mountain trails of that island. It is one of the few native hibiscus that is a true rainforest plant. One· of Hawai'i's most variable rainforest plants is **manono** (*Hedyotis terminalis*; E, 65; until recently put in the genus *Gouldia*). It can be a low-growing viny shrub in East Maui or a small tree along Kaua'i's Alaka'i Swamp Trail. It has small trumpet-shaped flowers that are usually purple on the outside and green on the inside. The soft half-inch fruits are round, usually shiny, and purple to black.

Confined to Maui and Hawai'i is an even lower growing shrub called **'ilihia** (*Cyrtandra platyphylla*; E, 38), related to African violets. The individual leaves are disproportionately large for such a small plant. 'Ilihia can be easily seen around Thurston Lava Tube.

'ilihia

'ie'ie

pāwale

Lianas and Vines

🐾 Worldwide, one of the most prominent features of tropical rainforest is the presence of huge woody vines called lianas (the "Tarzan transportation system"). In Hawai'i, however, such large vines are rare. About the only species that really qualifies is **climbing screwpine** or **'ie'ie** (*Freycinetia arborea*; I, 83) that grows at lower elevations in all Hawaiian rainforests. It is especially conspicuous in forests of Kona on the Big Island and along ridges in O'ahu's Ko'olau Mountains. In places, it forms dense, almost impenetrable tangles. In others it climbs high into the forest canopy on the trunks of koa and 'ōhi'a trees. The flowers and fruits form at the ends of stems surrounded by red or yellow bracts. Many visitors mistake these clusters for bromeliads, which do not grow wild in Hawai'i. One of the few other large lianas in Hawaiian forests is **climbing sorrel** or **pāwale** (*Rumex*

maile

ho'i kuahiwi

giganteus; E, 60), related to such mainland weeds as sheep sorrel and dock. As such it is another example, like the lobeliads discussed above, of the phenomenon of "insular woodiness." It has dense flower clusters and small dry fruits that look rather like a mass of red oatmeal. Pàwale also grows unsupported as a shrub in subalpine habitats.

Smaller vines are better represented in Hawaiian forests than lianas. Probably the most famous is **maile** (*Alyxia oliviformis*; E, 5), which holds a prominent place in Hawai'i's culture and traditions. Maile has a milky sap with a pungent aroma that many find pleasant. A maile lei can be dried to perfume an entire room. The green leaf leis are made as a stole rather than as a necklace and are worn at such occasions as weddings. Maile flowers are inconspicuous but it has fairly large oblong dark fruits. A vine that may look familiar to mainlanders is **hoi kuahiwi** (*Smilax melastomifolia*; E, 85), a relative of catbrier and greenbrier. However, like many Hawaiian plants, it has entirely lost the thorns of its ancestors. Hoi kuahiwi is a beautiful plant with thick leathery leaves that are usually red or purple when young. It has small white flowers and half-inch round white fruits.

VIII. Native Lowland Dry Forest

Pu'u Wa'a Wa'a, Hawai'i.

BEFORE THE COMING OF MAN, THE LEEWARD SIDES OF THE HAWAIIAN ISLANDS SUPPORTED A SPECIES-RICH DRY FOREST. TODAY, THAT HABITAT HAS VIRTUALLY DISAPPEARED. THE POLYNESIANS CLEARED OR BURNED SOME AREAS FOR AGRICULTURE, GRAZING ANIMALS BROUGHT BY EUROPEANS CONVERTED OTHERS TO PASTURE, AND CLEARING AND IRRIGATION MADE SUGAR CANE AND PINEAPPLE FIELDS OUT OF MOST OF THE REST. ONLY TATTERED SHREDS OF THIS ECOSYSTEM SURVIVE ON MOST ISLANDS, AND ONLY IN A FEW TINY POCKETS ON MAUI AND HAWAI'I CAN ANYTHING RESEMBLING THE ORIGINAL ECOSYSTEM BE GLIMPSED. ONE SUCH AREA IS ALONG MAMALAHOA HIGHWAY IN THE VICINITY OF PU'U WA'A WA'A; ANOTHER IS THE COASTAL PORTION OF HAWAII VOLCANOES NATIONAL PARK. MANY OF THE CHARACTERISTIC SPECIES OF THIS COMMUNITY ARE RARE BUT STILL SURVIVE AS SCATTERED INDIVIDUALS IN DISTURBED HABITATS (SECTIONS I-II); OTHERS NOW EXIST PRIMARILY IN BOTANICAL GARDENS AND ARBORETUMS. A PRECIOUS FEW ARE STILL COMMON.

COMMON TREES

🐦 Perhaps not surprisingly, one of the dominant trees of this open forest, as well as several other native ecosystems, is the highly variable **'ōhi'a-lehua** (*Metrosideros polymorpha*; E, 51), already discussed in Sections VI and VII. Slightly more common is **Hawaiian persimmon** or **lama** (*Diospyros sandwicensis*; E, 31). Like 'ōhi'a, lama has small leaves and many observers pass it by as "more of the same" when the two are growing together. Lama has a denser, more rounded crown than the scraggly 'ōhi'a and, of course, it lacks the red flowers. The inch-long persimmon-like fruits are red or orange. The dry forest tree most easily spotted at a distance is **wiliwili** (*Erythrina sandwicensis*; E, 36) with its thick trunk often tinged orange by lichens. The leaves are broad and rounded, and are the Hawaiian namesake (*lau-wiliwili*=wiliwili leaf) of butterflyfishes (*Chaetodon* and *Forcipiger*), common reef fishes in Hawai'i. (Despite the notoriety of humuhumu-nukunuku-a-pua'a, the longest Hawaiian fish name is actually lau-wiliwili-nukunuku-'oi'oi for *F. longirostris*). Wiliwili loses its leaves during the drier summer months, and produces yellow, yellow-green, or orange flowers before they return. Wiliwili's coral red seeds are released as the pods dry and curl. Wiliwili is common around Pu'u Wa'a Wa'a as

'ōhi'a growing in dry forest, South Kohala District, Hawai'i.

lama

Isolated **wiliwili** tree, Pu'u 'Anahulu, Hawai'i.

Flowers of **wiliwili**.

Pods and red seeds of **wiliwili**.

well as along the lower part of Koke'e Road in the first canyon above Kekaha, Kaua'i. Hawai'i shares **alahe'e** (*Canthium odoratum*; I, 65) with Micronesia and other islands of the South Pacific. Alahe'e has glossy green oval leaves that almost never come to a sharp point at the tip. The inconspicuous white flowers produce black fleshy fruits.

'alahe'e

kulu'ī

'āla'a

pāpala kepau

mahoe

RARER TREES AND SHRUBS

🌸 Many members of this community are now rare in the wild. Fortunately, a few such as the silvery-leaved shrub **kulu'ī** (*Nototrichium sandwicense*; E, 3), are gaining popularity as ornamentals. Kulu'ī has unusual dangling flower clusters with green bracts that look like tiny versions of the flower heads of white shrimp plant (Section V). The rusty-leaved **'āla'a** (*Pouteria sandwicensis*; E, 69), which was discussed in detail in Section VI, can also be found in dry forest where it usually has somewhat smaller leaves. Its football-shaped nut-like fruits are usually yellow but may occasionally be black. Look for it near Pu'u Wa'a Wa'a. Several rare dry forest species have peculiar distributions with inexplicable gaps. **Pāpala kepau** (*Pisonia brunoniana*; I, 52) is found from Australia to Hawai'i, where it is rare on most islands and absent from Kaua'i. It has comparatively large, broad, papery leaves and the flowers and unusual flattened key-like fruits growing in open clusters at the ends of branches. It can be found in temperate mixed forest as well as dry forest. A different distribution is shown by **mahoe** (*Alectryon macrococcus*; E, 68), which was found on all the larger islands except for Lana'i and Hawai'i, but is now endangered. It has compound leaves with blunt-tipped leaflets. Mahoe is related to the soapberries, which likewise have odd distributions (see also Section VI). One of them, **O'ahu soapberry** or **'aulu** (*Sapindus oahuensis*; E, 68), is confined to dry forest on that one island. It is also unusual in being the only member of its widespread genus with simple leaves. Although now rare in the wild, it is often planted in parks and gardens. Also confined to a single island is **Hawai'i halapepe** (*Pleomele hawaiiensis*; E, 78) which differs from its sister species on Kaua'i (Section VI) in its dry forest habitat. In growth form, Hawai'i halapepe will remind Californians of the Joshua tree. It is most conspicuous along Mamalahoa Highway between Huehue Ranch and Pu'u Wa'a Wa'a.

Hawai'i's native hibiscus reached their greatest diversity in the dry forests. Sadly, most of them are now endangered species, including the official State Flower, **ma'o hau hele** (*Hibiscus brackenridgei*; E, 44), a shrub with showy yellow flowers. It was found on all islands, but do not expect to find it in the wild today. Waimea Falls Park on O'ahu has many examples under cultivation, and it can also be seen at Manu Kā State Park, Hawai'i, and in front of Koke'e Museum, Kaua'i. Also at Manu Kā as well as elsewhere in Kona, one can also occasionally find cultivated examples of the spectacular red-flowered **hau hele 'ula**

O'ahu soapberry/'aulu

Hawai'i halapepe

(*Kokia drynarioides*; E, 44), now nearly extinct in the wild. It fell victim to grazing animals and habitat change. It is related to typical hibiscus, but note that its petals are partly rolled into a curved tube, possibly as an adaptation to bird pollination. Equally rare is the smaller **ko'oloa 'ula** (*Abutilon menziesii*; E, 44) that once lived in dry habitats on Maui, Lana'i, and Hawai'i but is now mostly known as a garden plant.

ma'o hau hele

hau hele 'ula

ko'oloa 'ula

IX. MONTANE DRY FOREST AND SUBALPINE SCRUB

Mamane/naio forest. Pu'u La'au, Hawai'i.

IN CONTRAST TO LOWLAND DRY FOREST, DRY FORESTS AT HIGHER ELEVATIONS IN THE HAWAIIAN ISLANDS ARE STILL PRESENT AS A RECOGNIZABLE ECOSYSTEM DESPITE THE PRESENCE OF MANY WEEDS. THESE FORESTS ARE RESTRICTED TO MAUI AND HAWAI'I BECAUSE THE OTHER ISLANDS DO NOT REACH SUFFICIENTLY HIGH ELEVATIONS. EACH ISLAND HAS ENDEMIC SPECIES IN THESE ZONES, BUT MOST ARE SHARED BETWEEN THEM.

mamane

naio

mountain sandalwood

MAMANE/NAIO FOREST

🦋 On the leeward slopes of Mauna Kea, and across the saddle between that mountain and Mauna Loa, grows a distinctive open forest dominated by two bushy trees. **Mamane** (*Sophora chrysophylla*; E, 36) has down-curving pale green compound leaves with small oval leaflets and pea-like golden yellow flowers. Its green ridged seed pods provide food for the Palila, an endangered finchlike Hawaiian honeycreeper found only in this forest. **Bastard sandalwood** or **naio** (*Myoporum sandwicense*; E, 48) has darker green simple leaves that often look slightly twisted, inconspicuous white or pinkish flowers, and soft, white, half-inch fruits. Both of these trees are found on Maui and other islands, but they are not dominant anywhere else. This clearly defined community is a Big Island specialty. Mamane and naio account for at least 99% of the trees in this forest. Although a few cinder cones harbor 'ōhi'a and koa, the only other large tree normally present in mamane/naio forest is a true sandalwood. **Mountain sandalwood** or **'ili'ahi** (*Santalum paniculatum*; E, 67) has dark green simple leaves more oval than those of naio and not twisted. The green 4-petaled flowers are in tight clusters at the ends of branches. Especially along the Saddle Road, two shrubs

are almost as abundant as the trees.
ʻĀheahea (*Chenopodium oahuense*; E,
24) is widespread in dry habitats but
is especially common here. Its
generic name means "goose foot,"
a reference to the peculiar shape of
the silvery leaves. Also widespread
in dry habitats of all islands is
Hawaiian hopseed or **ʻaʻaliʻi**
(*Dodonaea viscosa*; E, 68) whose
papery red seed pods are much
more conspicuous than its flowers.
These unusual fruits remain on the
plants for a long time. ʻAʻaliʻi has
simple leaves that often ascend
vertically from branches. Outside
the mamane/naio forest, it is common along the Mauna Loa Road in
Hawaii Volcanoes National Park and
on Haleakalā, Maui. **Small-leaf
mint** (*Stenogyne microphylla*; E, 41) is
a native woody vine that forms
dense masses in the interior of
large mamane or naio trees. It has
tiny leaves, smaller than the individual leaflets of mamane, and
straight tubular flowers that are
white inside and pink or yellow outside. It is easily the most distinctive
member of its genus (most
Stenogyne are rainforest herbs) but
had no Hawaiian name. It has
square stems but lacks the mint fra-
grance often found in the family.
These days, the most conspicuous
vine in mamane-naio forest is a
weed called **German ivy** (*Senecio
mikanoides*; A, 9), which is becoming
a major pest. Surprisingly, it is a

ʻāheahea

ʻaʻaliʻi

Flowering **ʻaʻaliʻi**

small-leaf mint

German ivy leaves and fruits

member of the daisy family. It has ivy-like leaves and inconspicuous fuzzy-looking yellow flowers, but the spikey ball-shaped fruit clusters are very noticeable.

HALEAKALĀ SCRUB

🐦 Between the upper limit of wet forests and the barren alpine zone on Maui is a fascinating subalpine scrub community, a major part of which has been preserved relatively intact in Haleakala National Park. It cannot be called a forest because only a few of its woody plants grow taller than the average human. Mamane is an important element, but here it usually grows smaller than in the Big Island forest described above. The only real tree is the beautiful red-flowered **Haleakalā sandalwood** or **'ili'ahi** (*Santalum haleakalae*; E, 67), which grows only here. It is rare, but several individuals grow next to the road above park headquarters and along the entrance road to Hosmer Grove. Prominent

German ivy in full bloom

Haleakala sandalwood

pukiawe

among the shrubs are both 'āheahea and 'a'ali'i. Joining them is **pukiawe** (*Styphelia tameiameae*; I, 33), an unusual shrub with tiny stiff leaves that grow all around the stem. This pattern gives the plant, at a distance, the look of a conifer like cedar or cypress. Pukiawe has inedible dry porcelain-like berries that may be red, pink, or white. It is a remarkable plant that grows in the understory of wet rainforest as well as in dry forest and subalpine scrub of Maui and Hawai'i, but it is nowhere so conspicuous as on Haleakalā. Often growing with pukiawe, but with edible berries, is **'ōhelo 'ai** (*Vaccinium reticulatum*; E, 34; formerly considered a separate species *V. berberidifolium*, now a variety). The Maui form differs from the Hawai'i one (Section X) mainly in having leaves that are often toothed on the edge, but this is a variable feature on both islands. 'Ōhelo 'ai is rare on Kaua'i, O'ahu, and Moloka'i. Especially conspicuous in the Haleakalā scrub is **subalpine pilo** (*Coprosma montana*; E, 65) with its bright orange berries crowded along the stems among the small opposite leaves. (See Section VII for more information about pilo as a group.)

Haleakalā shrubs that lack conspicuous fruits include **Maui na'ena'e** (*Dubautia menziesii*; E, 9), a member of the group that includes the silversword (Section X). Although it looks nothing like silversword,

'ōhelo 'ai

subalpine pilo

Maui na'ena'e

Maui wormwood

silver geranium/hinahina

Haleakala geranium/nohoanu

Hawai'i na'ena'e, Mauna Kea form

Hawai'i na'ena'e, Mauna Loa form

natural hybrids between them sometimes occur. Na'ena'e has stiff concave leaves that grow in 4 crowded ranks along the stem. The yellow flowers are borne in clusters at the branch tips and produce seeds with fluffy hairs for wind dispersal. **Maui wormwood** or **āhinahina** (*Artemisia mauiensis*; E, 9), related to sagebrush, has similar yellow flowers but an entirely different leaf form. It has the same Hawaiian name, which means silvery, as silversword because both have leaves covered with fine hairs as an adaptation to the strong high elevation sunlight. Wormwood leaves are finely divided and feathery, and at least faintly retain the sage aroma of mainland relatives.

Rounding out the Haleakalā shrub community are two interesting species of geranium that present yet another example of insular woodiness. **Silver geranium** or **hinahina** (*Geranium cuneatum*; E, 37) is more common in drier areas at higher elevations, and also grows in similar places on Mauna Loa, Hawai'i. Like many plants of this community, it has silvery leaves. Its 5-petaled flowers are yellowish white. **Haleakalā geranium** or **nohoanu** (*Geranium multiflorum*; E, 37) has lovely purple-striped pink or white flowers. Its leaves are green rather than silvery and larger than those of silver geranium. It grows at the upper edge of rainforest and in gulches higher up the mountain, and nowhere else.

SUBALPINE HAWAI'I

🐾 The Big Island of Hawai'i has 3 peaks high enough to support subalpine vegetation. However, the scrub habitat is actually more widespread than that because areas at lower elevations, such as Kilauea Volcano and old lava flows islandwide, mimic the subalpine conditions. The community here is similar to that on Haleakalā, with 'a'ali'i, pukiawe, and silver geranium prominent among the shrubs. Other species are similar to relatives on Maui, but endemic to Hawai'i. **Hawai'i na'ena'e** (*Dubautia ciliolata*; E, 9) is more variable than its Maui cousin and has 2 distinct subspecies. Mauna Kea plants (D. *c. glutinosa*) with heavy, ranked leaves look rather like the Haleakalā species. Plants in the Kilauea/Mauna Loa area (D. *c.ciliolata*) have smaller leaves that tend to encircle the branch rather than growing in ranks. **Kilauea pilo** (*Coprosma menziesii*; E, 65) resembles the Maui species but is much less abundant and has redder berries. Look for it along Chain of Craters Road. Another Big Island specialty is **huahekili uka** (*Scaevola kilaueae*; E, 39), one of the montane species (for the others see Section VII) that evolved from beach naupa-

Kilauea pilo

huahekili uka

ka. It resembles its rainforest relatives but has more leathery leaves and flowers with elongated tubular bases. Huahekili uka grows mostly around Kilauea Volcano.

X. LAVA FLOWS, ALPINE ZONES, AND CLIFF FACES

Young silverswords in rocky alpine zone, Haleakalā, Maui.

ACTIVE VOLCANISM IS TODAY CONFINED TO THE ISLAND OF HAWAI'I. WHEN THEY FIRST COOL, LAVA FLOWS ARE STERILE. RAIN BEGINS THE PROCESS OF BREAKDOWN OF THE HARD LAVA AND WIND BLOWS DUST THAT COLLECTS AS POCKETS OF SOIL HERE AND THERE. ONCE A FEW SMALL PLANTS GAIN A FOOTHOLD, IT IS ONLY A MATTER OF TIME UNTIL A FULL PLANT COMMUNITY DEVELOPS. IN HAWAI'I THE PIONEERS INCLUDE NOT ONLY THE EXPECTED LICHENS, FERNS, AND SMALL FLOWERING PLANTS, BUT ALSO A FEW HARDY VINES, SHRUBS, AND EVEN TREES.

🌺 Perhaps the most surprising element in this community is **'ōhi'a-lehua** (*Metrosideros polymorpha*; E, 51). These remarkable trees are early colonizers of lava and even bloom when only a few inches tall. Also conspicuous on fresh lava is the tree fern **ama'uma'u** (*Sadleria cyatheoides*; E, F3), for which the Kilauea "fire pit"

Halema'uma'u is named. It has a prominent place in Hawaiian folklore as one of the manifestations of the pig god Kamapua'a. The red-tinged young fronds are said to show the effects of proximity to Pele's fire. Other woody plants form sprawling mats on the lava. One of the most common is **kupaoa** (*Dubautia scabra*; E, 9) which is

Lava flow with pioneer **ʻōhiʻa**.

kukaenene

ʻōhelo ʻai

 amaʻumaʻu

kupaoa

probably the closest to the ancestral species of all the members of its genus. It has small white flowers borne on tall stems above the leaves. Also forming mats with its intertwining viny stems is **kukaenene** (*Coprosma ernodioides*; E, 65), a relative of pilo that has shiny black fruits. These are a favored food of the Nene or Hawaiian Goose, which effectively disperses the seeds. Nene also eat **ʻōhelo ʻai** (*Vaccinium reticulatum*; E, 34), which brightens the black lava with its colorful leaves and berries. Humans also like this ʻōhelo, whose fruit is more flavorful (the Hawaiian name means "edible ʻōhelo") than that of other Hawaiian huckleberries. The Big Island form of this species tends to

lava sorrel/pāwale

Early growth stage of **silversword**.

Blooming **silversword** with last year's skeleton.

have leaves with smooth edges and variably colored, often yellow, fruits. A rather large open shrub is **lava sorrel** or **pāwale** (*Rumex skottsbergii*; E, 60). It is restricted to southern parts of the Big Island and resembles its wet-forest relative (Section VII) except that its fruits are green, never red, and it is never a vine.

The harshest life zone of all in the Hawaiian Islands is found on the 4 highest mountaintops (Mauna Kea, Mauna Loa, Hualālai, and Haleakalā). These places are windswept, cold, and rocky, with little soil to hold what moisture there is, so are functionally deserts with little plant life. None of the alpine plants qualify as trees, and even the shrubs tend to be prostrate stragglers from the adjacent scrub zone. Nevertheless, in this harsh context grows what may be the crowning glory of Hawaiian plant evolution, the spectacular **silversword** or **āhinahina** (*Argyroxiphium sandwicense*; E, 9). It is the extreme example of an adaptive radiation from an ancestral tarweed that has also produced the various species of *Dubautia* and *Wilkesia*. Although still an endangered species, the silversword is recovering nicely in Haleakala National Park now that feral goats have been controlled. However, the tiny population on Mauna Kea, Hawai'i, is barely hanging on. Despite its yucca-like appearance, silversword is a composite, as its purple daisy-like flowers attest. It produces its huge flowering spike only once after growing for perhaps 20 years, then dies.

The root system is very shallow and spreads just under the surface for a large area around the plant, so approaching a silversword too closely can damage its roots. If you want a close-up picture, stay on trails and use a telephoto lens.

Exposed cliff faces resemble lava flows and alpine zones in the challenges they pose for plant life, but can be found on islands such as Moloka'i, O'ahu, and Kaua'i that lack these other habitats. A few plants have adapted to this very specific habitat. **Hawaiian wormwood** or **āhinahina** (*Artemisia australis*; E, 9) resembles its subalpine Maui relative (above) but is found on cliff faces on all islands. It can be most easily seen along the old road below the Pali Overlook on Oahu. Its leaves have slightly broader, less delicate lobes than Maui wormwood and are more likely to have a strong sage aroma. Perhaps the most peculiar plant in Hawaii is **ōlulu** (*Brighamia insignis*; E, 16), which grows on sea cliffs of Kaua'i and Ni'ihau, with a related species on Moloka'i. Although it resembles a cabbage on a thick pedestal, it is actually the most highly evolved representative of the lobeliads, a group that exhibits adaptive radiation in Hawaii (see Section VII). Both species of *Brighamia* are now endangered and unlikely to be seen in the wild. Plants are being cultivated for propagation at Kilauea Point National Wildlife Refuge on Kaua'i.

Closeup of **silversword** flowers.

Hawaiian wormwood/āhinahina

ōlulu

APPENDIX 1:
GARDEN TREES AND FLOWERS

This book is a guide to wild plants. Often, however, one cannot tell whether a plant is wild or planted. This is particularly true in overgrown sites that may have been previously cultivated or landscaped. Also, many wild plants have close relatives that are so common in parks and gardens that comparison is necessary for identification. This appendix will help observers eliminate garden plants from those growing wild, and provide quick comparisons with close relatives. It is basically a picture gallery of ornamentals and agricultural plants commonly seen in Hawai'i. The individual plants are not discussed. Each is labelled with vernacular and scientific names and the number of its family. They are presented in 2 groups: flowering trees and shrubs grouped more or less by flower color; and fruit and foliage plants. For detailed treatment of garden plants, one can consult any of a variety of books devoted primarily to them (see For Further Information).

FLOWERING TREES AND SHRUBS

**Indian coralbean/
wiliwili haole**
Erythrina variegata 36

bottlebrush
Callistemon citrinus 51

pink tecoma
Tabebuia rosea 11

St. Thomas orchid tree
Bauhinia monandra 36

bougainvillea
Bougainvillea sp. 52

crape-myrtle
Lagerstroemia indica 43

jatropha
Jatropha integerrima 35

flame-of-the-wood
Ixora casei 65

cock's-comb coral tree
Erythrina crista-galli 36

geiger tree/kou haole
Cordia sebestena 13

cape honeysuckle
Tecomaria capensis 11

sunburst pincussion protea
Leucospermum cordifolium 61

chenille plant
Acalypha hispida 35

Mexican plumeria (red)
Plumeria rubra 5

Mexican plumeria (yellow)
Plumeria rubra 5

allamanda
Allamanda cathartica 5

spray-of-gold
Galphinia gracillis

lollipop plant
Pachystachys lutea 36

Siamese cassia
Cassia siamea 36

yellow hybrid hibiscus
Hibiscus x *rosa-sinensis* 44

golden trumpet tree
Tabebuia serratifolia 11

silver trumpet tree
Tabebuia aurea 11

golden-shower tree
Cassia fistula 36

Singapore plumeria
Plumeria obtusa 5

Tahitian gardenia/tiare
Gardenia taitensis 65

Cherokee rose
Rosa laevigata 64

hydrangea
Hydrangea macrophylla 40

blue vitex
Vitex trifolia 75

blue ginger
Dichorisandra thyrsifolia

Burmese rosewood
Pterocarpus indicus 36

date palm
Phoenix dactylatra 80

banyan
Ficus bengalensis 47

large-leaf fig
Ficus macrophylla 47

weeping fig
Ficus benjamina 47

loquat
Eriobotrya japonica 63

lychee
Litchi chinensis 68

monstera
Monstera deliciosa 79

pineapple
Ananas comosus

banana
Musa xparadisiaca 82

pencil tree
Euphorbia tirucalli 35

traveler's tree
Ravenala madagascariensis

APPENDIX 2:
FORESTRY CONIFERS AND SIMILAR TREES

Forestry project, Polipoli Springs, Maui.

Like Appendix 1, this one is a simple portrait gallery. Conifers, also called cone-bearing trees, evergreens, and gymnosperms, are a group of trees that do not readily fit any of the other categories used herein. They are poor island colonizers and none ever reached the Hawaiian Islands naturally. Many species have, however, been planted in large reforestation projects or as ornamentals. Many of them grow well in Hawai'i, but others suffer from the absence of a cold winter and grow in abnormal ways. The trees are an important element in the Hawaiian landscape and often produce seedlings, but they rarely spread beyond the original plantation and, with the possible exception of "Norfolk Island Pine" (Section V), few can be said to be truly naturalized in Hawai'i. However, Mexican weeping pine shows evidence of becoming established and is a potential pest in Hosmer Grove on Maui. This historic forestry plantation is obvious along the road just outside the upper entrance to Haleakala National Park. Before the park was established, the grove was planted as an experiment to find out which alien trees were most suitable for reforestation in Hawai'i (in those days native trees were not considered). Today, Hosmer Grove is a virtual museum of introduced conifers. Other important forestry plantations can be seen in the Koke'e area on Kaua'i and near Polipoli Springs on Maui. Also shown are 2 species of ironwood (*Casuarina*) related to the widespread species

(Section I) but found mostly in planted groves. Although often mistaken for them, they are not conifers but flowering plants placed in their own distinctive family. Unlike conifers, casuarinas are good island colonizers, mostly native to the southwest Pacific. Several other species have been planted in Hawaii, and they often hybridize so sorting them out is best left to the botanists.

sugi
Cryptomeria japonica C4

Port-Orford cedar
Chamaecyparis lawsonianus C2

Mexican weeping pine
Pinus patula C3

slash pine
Pinus elliottii C3

redwood
Sequoia sempervirens C4

Monterey cypress
Cupressus macrocarpus C2

parana-pine
Araucaria angustifolia C1

longleaf ironwood
Casuarina glauca

river-oak ironwood
Casuarina cunninghamiana

APPENDIX 3:

PLANT FAMILIES NUMBERED IN THE TEXT

FLOWERING PLANTS

Dicots

1.	ACANTHACEAE	Acanthus Family
2.	AIZOACEAE	Sea-purslane Family
3.	AMARANTHACEAE	Amaranth Family
4.	ANACARDIACEAE	Sumac/Mango Family
5.	APOCYNACEAE	Dogbane Family
6.	AQUIFOLIACEAE	Holly Family
7.	ARALIACEAE	Ginseng/Ivy Family
8.	ASCLEPIADACEAE	Milkweed Family
9.	ASTERACEAE	Sunflower/Daisy/Composite Family
10.	BATACEAE	Saltwort Family
11.	BIGNONIACEAE	Trumpetflower Family
12.	BIXACEAE	Annotto Family
13.	BORAGINACEAE	Heliotrope Family
14.	BUDDLEIACEAE	Butterfly-bush Family
15.	CACTACEAE	Cactus Family
16.	CAMPANULACEAE	Lobelia Family
17.	CANNABACEAE	Hemp Family
18.	CAPRIFOLIACEAE	Honeysuckle/Elder Family
19.	CARICACEAE	Papaya Family
20.	CARYOPHYLLACEAE	Pink Family
21.	CASUARINACEAE	Ironwood Family
22.	CECROPIACEAE	Cecropia Family
23.	CELASTRACEAE	Bittersweet Family
24.	CHENOPODIACEAE	Goosefoot Family
25.	CLUSIACEAE	Mangosteen Family
26.	COMBRETACEAE	Indian Almond Family
27.	CONVOLVULACEAE	Morning-glory Family
28.	CORYNOCARPACEAE	Karakanut Family
29.	CUCURBITACEAE	Melon/Gourd Family
30.	CUSCUTACEAE	Dodder Family
31.	EBENACEAE	Ebony Family
32.	ELAEOCARPACEAE	Elaeocarpus Family
33.	EPACRIDACEAE	Epacris Family
34.	ERICACEAE	Heath Family
35.	EUPHORBIACEAE	Spurge Family
36.	FABACEAE	Pea Family
37.	GERANIACEAE	Geranium Family
38.	GESNERIACEAE	African Violet Family
39.	GOODENIACEAE	Scaevola Family
40.	HYDRANGEACEAE	Hydrangea Family
41.	LAMIACEAE	Mint Family
42.	LAURACEAE	Laurel Family
43.	LYTHRACEAE	Loosestrife Family
44.	MALVACEAE	Mallow Family
45.	MELASTOMACEAE	Melastome Family
46.	MELIACEAE	Mahogany Family
47.	MORACEAE	Mulberry Family
48.	MYOPORACEAE	Naio Family
49.	MYRICACEAE	Bayberry Family
50.	MYRSINACEAE	Myrsine Family
51.	MYRTACEAE	Myrtle Family
52.	NYCTAGINACEAE	Four-o'clock Family
53.	OLEACEAE	Olive Family
54.	ONAGRACEAE	Evening Primrose Family
55.	PASSIFLORACEAE	Passionfruit Family
56.	PHYTOLACCACEAE	Pokeweed Family
57.	PIPERACEAE	Pepper Family
58.	PITTOSPORACEAE	Pittosporum Family
59.	PLUMBAGINACEAE	Leadwort Family
60.	POLYGONACEAE	Buckwheat Family
61.	PROTEACEAE	Protea Family
62.	RHAMNACEAE	Buckthorn Family

63. RHIZOPHORACEAE   Mangrove Family
64. ROSACEAE   Rose Family
65. RUBIACEAE   Coffee Family
66. RUTACEAE   Rue Family
67. SANTALACEAE   Sandalwood Family
68. SAPINDACEAE   Soapberry Family
69. SAPOTACEAE   Sapodilla Family
70. SOLANACEAE   Nightshade Family
71. STERCULIACEAE   Cacao Family
72. THYMELIACEAE   Akia Family
73. ULMACEAE   Elm Family
74. URTICACEAE   Nettle Family
75. VERBENACEAE   Verbena Family
76. VISCACEAE   Mistletoe Family
77. ZYGOPHYLLACEAE   Caltrop Family

Monocots

78. AGAVACEAE   Agave Family
79. ARACEAE   Arum Family
80. ARECACEAE   Palm Family
81. CYPERACEAE   Sedge Family
82. MUSACEAE   Banana Family
83. PANDANACEAE   Screw-pine Family

84. POACEAE   Grass Family
85. SMILACACEAE   Greenbrier Family
86. TYPHACEAE   Cattail Family

CONIFERS

C1. ARAUCARIACEAE   Araucaria Family
C2. CUPRESSACEAE   Cypress Family
C3. PINACEAE   Pine Family
C4. TAXODIACEAE   Redwood Family

FERNS AND FERN RELATIVES

F1. ASPIDIACEAE   Woodfern Family
F3. ASPLENIACEAE   Spleenwort Family
F3. BLECHNACEAE   Chain-fern Family
F4. DENNSTAEDTIACEAE   Bracken Family
F5. DICKSONIACEAE   Treefern Family
F7. ELAPHOGLOSSACEAE   Tongue-fern Family
F8. GLEICHENIACEAE   False Staghorn
    Family
F9. LYCOPODIACEAE   Clubmoss Family
F9. POLYPODIACEAE   Polypody Family

FOR FURTHER INFORMATION

BALDWIN, ROGER E. 1980. *Hawai'i's poisonous plants*. Hilo: Petroglyph Press, Ltd.

BORNHORST, HEIDI LEIANUENUE. 1996. *Growing Hawaiian native plants*. Honolulu: The Bess Press.

KEPLER, ANGELA KAY. 1984. *Hawaiian Heritage Plants*. Honolulu: Oriental Publishing Co. [An excellent guide to plants of significance to the history of Hawai'i.]

KEPLER, ANGELA KAY. 1990. *Trees of Hawai'i*. Honolulu: University of Hawai'i Press. [Good photographic coverage of native and introduced trees.]

KEPLER, ANGELA KAY. 1997. *Hawai'i's Floral Splendor*. Honolulu: Mutual Publishing. [Probably the best guide to garden plants with many native species as well.]

LAMB, SAMUEL H. 1981. *Native Trees and Shrubs of the Hawaiian Islands*. Santa Fe, NM: The Sunstone Press.

LAMOUREUX, CHARLES H. 1996. *Trailside Plants of Hawai'i's National Parks*. Revised Edition. Hawaii Volcanoes National Park: Hawaii Natural History Association.

LITTLE, E. L., AND R. G. SKOLMEN. 1989. *Common forest trees of Hawaii (native and introduced)*. U. S. Dept. Agriculture, Agriculture Handbook No. 690. [The only comprehensive coverage of conifers and other trees planted for forestry in Hawai'i.]

MERLIN, MARK. 1995. *Hawaiian Forest Plants*. Honolulu: Pacific Guide Books.

MERLIN, MARK. Undated. *Hawaiian Coastal Plants and Scenic Shorelines*. Honolulu: Oriental Publishing Co.

PERRY, F., and R. HAY. 1983. *A Field Guide to Tropical and Subtropical Plants*. New York: Van Nostrand Reinhold Co. [Covers plants widely planted throughout the world's tropical regions, including Hawai'i.]

ROCK, JOSEPH F. 1975. *The Indigenous Trees of the Hawaiian Islands*. Rutland, Vt. and Tokyo: Charles E. Tuttle Co. [A classic reference first published in 1913.]

SOHMER, S. H., and ROBERT GUSTAFSON. 1987. *Plants and Flowers of Hawai'i*. Honolulu: Univ. of Hawai'i Press. [A wonderfully well written and well illustrated book. Not a field guide, but recommended to anyone interested in native plant communities.]

VALIER, KATHY. 1995. *Ferns of Hawai'i*. Honolulu: University of Hawai'i Press. [The only guide available to Hawaiian ferns, but incomplete and difficult to use.]

WAGNER, W. L., D. R. HERBST, AND S. H. SOHMER. 1990. *Manual of the flowering plants of Hawai'i*. 2 vols. Univ. Hawai'i Press and Bishop Mus. Press, Honolulu. [The authoritative scholarly reference on the subject.]

INDEX